I was shown a path with footprints on it, and I heard the words, "Follow thou Me."

Sometimes that path was straight and smooth. At other times it was rough, very winding and difficult. At times the footprints seemed to disappear completely when there were obstacles to be overcome.

I still heard the words, "Follow thou Me. Be not concerned when there are obstacles; for every obstacle that is overcome strengthens your faith and belief in Me, your constant guide and companion."

FOOTPRINTS ON THE PATH

Eileen Caddy

Edited by Roy McVicar

Illustrated by Jane Crosen

FINDHORN

© Eileen Caddy 1976
First published 1976
Second impression 1979
Second edition 1981
Second impression 1985
Third impression 1987
Fourth impression 1988
ISBN 0 905249 54 2

Set in 10/12 Univers by Findhorn Publications
Printed and bound by John G. Eccles, Inverness
Published by The Findhorn Press,
Findhorn, Moray, Scotland

CONTENTS

Footprints in snow,
Footprints in snow.
Where do you come from,
Where do you go?

—from a poem by Stephen Field
which befriended the illustrations

The inspirational writings in this book had their origin as Eileen Caddy, co-founder of the Findhorn Community, listened to the voice of the God within. Many years ago that voice had come to her at a time of great uncertainty and unhappiness, and through the years it has been her constant guide and stimulus and hope.

The messages here offer, to those who will read them receptively, nothing less than a way of living which can be more meaningful, more purposeful, and result in a more worthwhile contribution to life.

They may be deceptive in their simplicity. If you look in them for either beautiful spiritual sentiments or profound philosophic truths, you will miss their real value for you and in so doing you will miss a wealth of life and love and wisdom.

For their very simplicity can be their greatest challenge. No matter how advanced you may be on the spiritual path, there is on every page, almost in every line, a challenge concerning your way of life, your way of living, the actual expression or demonstration of your inward spiritual state.

The messages cannot be classified, for they are living truths which are as complex and varied as life itself.

They should therefore not be read like ordinary devotional talks or sermonettes because they are not these. There is only one way in which to read them, and that is first to make up your mind that either they are in fact how Eileen has picked up what God was saying to her and through her, or else they are not worth your time to read.

But if you can be open to their divine origin, then they can be a unique and wonderful thing for you: they can be as a mirror in which to look at yourself.

Read each sentence as being spoken to you, and applying to you. See where it does apply, and what steps you can then take in the light of what it has shown.

If you will do this, taking the messages one at a time, then each one can open another window in your soul towards eternity. Each one will enable you to make your life richer and fuller and happier and more effective in service. Each one will be another step towards realizing some of your fondest hopes for your own life, and even more important towards attaining the highest potential of which you are capable—God's supreme purpose for your life.

In other words, these messages can be as "footprints on the path" which leads you home to God.

Roy McVicar

AWARENESS

I was aware of a tremendous increase of light. It seemed to spread out gradually like the glorious sunrise.

I heard the words: "My light is always there. Become more and more aware of it and of its full power and glory."

Then I saw before me in great letters of fire the word AWARENESS.

Wake up and live.

Set your sights high,
              the higher the better.
Expect the most wonderful things to happen,
              not in the future but right now.
Realize that nothing is too good.
Allow absolutely nothing to hamper you
              or hold you up in any way.

Be enthusiastic about life;
    it is a wonderful life,
       make it so by your enthusiasm.

Learn to be very clear and definite about what you desire in life;
never be vague or uncertain.
    You can do all things,
    you can be all things to all men
    when your faith and trust are in Me.
Have confidence in your ability to do all things
    because you are drawing your substance,
    your all from Me.
I am your all in all.

Stride forward with a firm steady step,
knowing with a deep
                        certain
                           inner knowing
that you will reach every goal you set yourselves,
that you will achieve every aim.

Start doing this today.
Why put off until tomorrow what you know you can do today?
    Far too many souls procrastinate
    or suffer from inertia,
    with the result that nothing gets done;
and they go on vaguely hoping
    that one day something will happen to change their lives,
    that perhaps circumstances will take a hand,

and then everything will fall into place for them.
It is not the way to live a full and glorious life—
in a vague and dreaming fashion.

Why not take positive action?
    Why not start the wheels turning?
        Once you have done your part you will receive all the help you need,
            but not until then.
I help those who help themselves,
    not those who sit back hoping that something will happen
        but fail to take any action.

You can soar to great heights
    with hearts filled with praise and thanksgiving;
but like the tiny lark, you have to take off from the ground,
you have to make that special effort.
    It need not be a strain,
        it can be a joyous light-hearted effort
           which is an effortless effort.

Once you are off the ground
    up and up you can go with complete freedom.
    Why remain anchored
when action on your part can change your lives completely?

When you desire something badly enough you will achieve it:
    you will allow nothing to stand in the way,
    you will never take "no" for an answer
    but will know you can do all things with Me.

The take-off of an aeroplane from the ground demands a special boost
of power;
Go within
and receive your special boost of power to set you on your way.

There is no greater power than My power
    and it is available to you
        at any time
            when you choose to draw from it.
I never withhold it from any
    who are ready
        who reach out for it
            and use it aright.
It is yours
    when you are ready.

You are surrounded by beauty everywhere.
Open your eyes
    and see it
        and give constant thanks for it.

Let the things of beauty transform you and inspire you
to your highest and best.
Beauty draws the very best out of and unites you
with the highest.

The beauty that is within you cannot be contained . . .
    it will be reflected without;
    let it shine forth.
    Fill your hearts and minds with beautiful thoughts and reflect Me
    for I am beauty.

Look for the beauty in everything,
and when you look deep enough and long enough you will see it.
Rise above the sordid ugly things in life, for by rising above them
you can help to transform and transmute them.
    Beauty is in the eye of the beholder,
        therefore it is deep within you.
Go forth this day determined to see beauty in everyone and everything
and you will do so.

Love and beauty go hand in hand.
So let My universal love flow freely in and through each one of you,
bringing unity and oneness.
As each one of you opens his heart and keeps the love flowing
this will come about;
for the more love there is between all of you
    the greater will be the unity and oneness.

I say to you over and over again, "Love one another."
    This does not mean that you are to tolerate one another,
        or try very hard to love one another;
but you will find when you open your hearts
    and can fill them with loving beautiful thoughts
        that you will want to love all those you come into contact with

no matter who they are.

This is the free flow of My universal love which knows no discrimination
and does not pick and choose who is going to be loved
and who is not.
My love is the same for each and every one.
How much you are willing to accept is up to you.

You can be infilled by My wondrous love,

or you can shut it out of your lives,

it is simply up to you.
It is always there waiting for you when you are ready for it.

This is what is taking place at this time.
There is a wonderful opening up and acceptance of My love
    which brings you all closer together,
        uniting you in oneness.

        Be not afraid to express this love;
        it is beyond the personality,
        it is of the very highest.

There is nothing possessive about it,
    for a possessive love stifles and kills;
        it shuts out My divine love.
My universal love grows and grows,
    it includes everyone,
        it possesses no one,
            and yet all are one in it,
                all feel part of it.
It enfolds all because it is the allness of all—all inclusive.

Learn to wear your heart on your sleeve
and never be ashamed to demonstrate your love for one another.

Love is the greatest uniting factor in the universe,
so Love
        Love
            Love.

Raise your consciousness.
Realize that you are ageless,
                you are as young as time,
                        as old as eternity.
As you live fully and gloriously in the ever present now,
    you are always as young as the present,
    you are constantly being reborn in spirit and in truth.

You cannot remain static in this spiritual life;
there is always something new and exciting to learn and to do.
Living in a state of expectancy keeps you ever alert and young.
When the mind becomes old and dull, life loses all its sparkle and zest.
Keep your minds alert and you can never grow old.

            The fountain of youth is your consciousness;
            the joy of living is the elixir of life.

Expect the very best in life and draw it to you.
For too long so many of you have accepted this in theory,
    but have failed to live it
        and demonstrate it.
Why not start doing something about it right now!
    Stop thinking about it
        and talking about it.
All the time I am urging you to live a life;
over and over again I ask you to live that life.
    If you are tired of hearing the same things repeated
        then why not do something about it?

Until these vitally important lessons are absorbed by each one
    and become part of you
    and they live and move and have their being in you,
    I have to go on repeating them.

When you teach a child to do something
    you may have to show that child the same thing many times,
    you may have to wait very patiently
while it fumbles around trying to do it on its own.
The child may appear to be all thumbs,

but unless you allow it to try
     it will never learn.
Simply watching you doing it all the time will not help the child
to learn for itself.
That is why life has to be lived for it to be really effective;
    and you have to live it,
no one else can live your life for you.

Always be willing to learn,
                to accept the new;
never close your mind and reject it because you cannot understand it.
Open yourselves up
    and allow the new to reveal itself
        and always be willing to go halfway.
A closed mind will get you nowhere
    for you cannot grow and expand when you close your mind.
There are always two sides to a picture;
learn to be tolerant,
try to see both sides.

        "Judge not that ye be not judged";
        condemn not that ye be not condemned.

Be a good listener.
Everyone likes a good listener.
Unless you take time to listen to what someone has to say
you can be of no help to that soul.

You will find that when you fail to understand some new truth with the mind,
    if you sit still
    and raise your consciousness
you will be able to get into tune with the infinite, universal mind
                and to become one with it,
                        with Me,
and you will be able to understand all things.

Rejoice
and give constant thanks
for the best is yet to come.

Day
   after
         day
I pour down upon you all My good and perfect gifts.
You are surrounded by all the best in life.
   So open your eyes
         and behold My wonders
               and realize how mightily blessed you are.

Cease bemoaning your lot in life,
   cease concentrating on the negative things in your lives;
         concentrate on all the wonderful things
         until they become reality
         until they become part of you.

Take off those blinkers,
see the miracles of life
and realize that you are part of it,
that you live and move and have your being in it.

Why not make a habit of approaching life in the right spirit,
   joyously,
   expectantly,
      with absolute faith that only the very best is for you?
Over and over again I have told you that I want only the very best for you.
Why can you not accept this
and cease accepting the second best?

I tell you any old thing will not do.
   If you choose to think in that half-hearted way
      you will draw any old thing to you,
            but this is not My will for you.
I want you to have all the very best in life
   and when you have learned to put first things first in your lives,
      all the very best will be yours
            because I know that you will use it for the good of the whole
                  and to My glory.

I do not want you to go through life with a heavy weight on your shoulders,
bowed down by the cares of the world.
I need you free

so that I can work in and through you.
   Stop being a worrier;
   cast all your cares and burdens upon Me
   for you help no one by worrying.

Where is your faith and belief?
Where does your security lie?
You must get your values straight.
What is the use of spending hours in meditation if you go through life
                           over-burdened?
   You must find the perfect balance in life,
   be able to raise your consciousness to great heights,
     then be able to bring it down into your everyday living.
Live a Life.

"The kingdom of heaven is within you."
It is right there waiting for you to recognize it.
   You must know this,
       believe it,
           then bring it about.
The kingdom of heaven is a state of mind
and it is for everyone to seek and find.

Every soul has to long for this before they can find it.
The desire must be there,
and the desire must be so strong that nothing will be allowed to stand
in the way.
You can bring about anything you really desire.
See that your every desire is of the very highest,
   that it will benefit the whole
   and not just your little self.
Let your minds be stayed on Me, then your desires will be pure and selfless.

Learn to discipline and control your thinking.
This is something to be achieved in life
though you may have great difficulty in doing this to begin with.
   Never give up,
       be patient,
           persevere;
and in the end you will be able to control and discipline your every
thought,
           word,
               and deed
and bring about the most wonderful results in your lives.

You will behold miracle upon miracle
because you are working with My laws
                    not against them.

The secret of making something work in your lives is,
        first of all, the deep desire to make it work:
        then the faith and belief that it can work:
        then to hold that clear definite vision in your consciousness
        and see it working out step by step,
        without one thought of doubt or disbelief.
Your positive attitude is vitally important to anything you undertake in life.
When you are determined to do something
        wholeheartedly,
            perfectly,
                and to do it with love
the results are bound to be wonderful.

Start right now to do everything that has to be done
with that right attitude and see what happens;
when you see everything working out in true perfection
never fail to give thanks
for gratitude keeps the door wide open
and enables more and more to work out in your lives.

It is when you start taking things for granted
        that all the joy goes out of life
            and the door begins to close.

Then the best thing to do
        and do quickly,
            is to stop
                and take time to count your blessings,

realize how mightily blessed you are
and then give thanks.
This works like magic in everyone's lives.
Why not try it next time life begins to appear dull,
uninteresting
and boring,
and see what a transformation it will make in every way

The sooner you realize that life is indeed what you make it
the more quickly will you behold the right results
and your whole attitude will take a change for the better.

You must all learn to be real optimists
and expect the very best in everything you undertake.
Know that you can and will do it perfectly,
    that there will be nothing slapdash in your work or in your lives.
Simply do it unto Me
    and to My glory
        and you are bound to do everything with love
            and therefore in true perfection.

This also applies to the way you look
                and the way you behave.

When you are doing everything for Me,
when your greatest desire is to do My will because of your love for Me,
    you will always want to do everything well;
        you will always want to look your best,
            give of your best,
                and you will never be satisfied with anything less
                    nor be half-hearted over anything.

It is necessary every now and again to take time
    and see where you need to change
        and then be willing to do so.
If you happen to have a blind spot
    be willing to have that blind spot revealed to you by someone else
        and never resent it
            for what is done in love can only be for the very best.

Learn to change
ınd change quickly
                without any pull back,
and know that every change is indeed for the very best.

Why not relax,
    let go
        and let Me take over;
for the more stress and strain there is in your lives the less you get done.

Why not let yourselves flow with nature,
    flow with the tide
        and do what has to be done quite simply, naturally and joyously.

Why not enjoy life,
    instead of going through it with grim determination,
        forcing yourselves to do this, that, or the other without any joy or love.

Life is really wonderful
    when your attitude towards it is right,
    and you are in harmony with it,
    and cease resisting everything.

Have I not told you,
when you long for something badly enough you can bring it about?
But, always see that your longing is for something that will benefit the whole
and cease trying to draw things to the self,
    for when your motives are selfish
        no good can come out of your longings.

When you undertake something,
                whatever it is,
do it wholeheartedly
           or not at all.
This is so vitally important.
So many souls do a job simply because they feel it has to be done
and then wonder why life is so drab and dull.

This is not living;
    this is merely existing,
        and is not the way I want you to live.
This is not the full and glorious life that I keep telling you about;
    the life that I have promised is your true heritage.
But if you fail to claim your true heritage

you have no one but yourselves to blame.

Claim that which is yours,
    give eternal thanks for it,
        and live and move and have your being in it.

Stop talking about it,
    stop hearing about it,
        simply accept it.
           It is so simple.

Why must you make everything so complicated for yourselves?
Why must you wear sackcloth and ashes when all My good and perfect gifts
are yours?

How foolish can you be,
    how blind and stubborn,
        refusing to accept the good and perfect which is yours?

How many go through life doing this,
    refusing to open their eyes
        and open their hearts,
and therefore failing to see My wonders and glories all around them?

Why not make today a special day:
    really see the very best in everything,
    give thanks for everything,
    enjoy everything as it should be enjoyed.

I want you to enjoy life,
                  so why not do so?
Start off by seeing the beauty of nature all around you,
    and you will find that one wonderful thing will lead to the next,
        until your whole life is one of wonderment and joy.

"Be ye transformed by the renewing of your minds."

   The more positive and constructive your thinking
   the smoother will be the running of your life.

Never forget:
what you put into your deeper mind is what will come out of it.
Therefore if you feed the mind with destructive
                              discontented
                                 dissatisfied
                                    inharmonious thoughts
those are the ones that will come out of it,
for that which goes in is bound to come out sooner or later.

When you fill yourself with things of the Spirit
     and function from the level of the Spirit
          that which is of the Spirit will reveal itself in your life and living.

Raise your consciousness,
     keep it raised,
          never drag it in the mud;
for the more mud and dirt you collect the more difficulty you will have
in ridding yourself of it.

          Walk in the light and radiate light.
          Fill your hearts with love and pour forth love.

Make a habit of dwelling on all the glorious things in life,
     of seeing the very best in everyone and everything.
          Refuse to dwell on the depressing things
               but raise your thinking,
let it soar higher and higher like the tiny lark
     and sing your song of praise and thanksgiving for all the wonderful
          things which are yours.

          The more grateful you are,
          the more positive you are,
          the higher you will soar.
It is the negative things which drag you down;
and the positive, constructive things which raise you higher and higher.

Never fail to give thanks for everything,
for every lesson you learn no matter how difficult it may be:
     realize that only the very best is bound to come out of it
          that every difficulty is but a stepping stone along the way.

There are important lessons which have to be learned
and the sooner you learn them the better.
Never try to shirk them
    or get round them
        but see them for what they are
            and face them fairly and squarely.

Surmount them and do it quickly,
speed is essential in overcoming,
there is so much waiting to be revealed to those who can overcome.

Never be like a gramophone needle that is stuck in a groove,
repeating the same old mistakes over and over again.
    It is not at all necessary,
    it is up to you to do something about it,
    nobody else can do it for you.

When you really want to change you can do it.
When you really want to be different
    and live a victorious life,
        you simply have to make up your mind that you are going to do it
            and you will do it.
Why not start right now
                    seeing the best in life
and so enjoy life
            as it should be enjoyed.

Do you find a real joy in the work you are doing,
                in the life you are living?
Do you find real pride in a job
                not only well done but perfectly done?
Do you dislike anything that is done
                shoddily or half-heartedly?

24

Is your heart so much in what you are doing,
are you so conscious of the fact that you are doing everything for Me
and to My honour and glory
that you cannot be satisfied with anything that is not "just so"?
This is as it should be;
    you should never be satisfied in a job half done
       or done in a half-hearted begrudging manner.
Do all that has to be done with joy and with love,
and let this include everything you do
from the most mundane job to those vitally important ones.

See that your attitude is right in everything you undertake so that
the right vibrations are put into it.

There are many souls who do not yet realize the importance of vibrations.
Because they are something that cannot be seen with the visible eye
they feel they do not really matter.

I tell you they are vitally important;
    for a job that is done wholeheartedly and with love
    carries with it something really tremendous
    and will be felt by anyone who is sensitive and aware of vibrations.
That is why your attitude to everything you undertake should be right.

Next time you take on a job you do not feel in harmony with
    take time to go away by yourself
    and get into harmony before you continue.
Do not think about yourself and how you feel
    but consider all those who may come into contact with what you do
    and how they are going to feel about it.
As you do this you will find your negative attitude will change
    and you will be able to do it in a completely different frame of mind.
What is more you will find yourself enjoying doing it
and it will no longer be a bind and a bore.

Learn to blend in,
to harmonize with all life,
to feel and to know the wonder of being at one and in tune with
everything you do, say, and think.

      The more you are aware of your oneness with Me
      the more you will be in tune with all life.

You have to get into tune;
it does not just happen, especially when you have been out of tune.

When a musical instrument is out of tune,
   time has to be taken to get it into tune again.
When you are out of tune,
    you have to take time to get into tune once again,
      so there is nothing in you that jars and strikes a discordant note.

Relax
and know that there is time for everything.

Everyone has an equal amount of time,
but it is how you use it that really matters.
   Do you use it to the full,
   and enjoy every moment of it,
   or do you dissipate time by failing to put first things first?
Why not first get your values right
and know without any doubt what you put first.

Cease being a slave to time.
Why not make it your servant instead,
   then it will never rule you but you will rule it?

Accept that you can only do one thing at a time,
   do it perfectly,
      and then move on to the next.

Never try to look too far ahead
   and exhaust yourselves doing so.
      You can only live one moment at a time.
If you try and plan too far ahead
   you may be very disappointed when things do not work out as you planned.

Many changes can take place in a very short space of time
   and in your planning you know not what those changes are
      and cannot account for them.

It is best to live in the moment fully
   and let the future take care of itself
       and unfold at the right time.

Every moment is precious
therefore never squander it in wrong thinking and wrong actions.
   Do what you know has to be done,
   and do it now,
   and do it knowing that only the very best will come out of it.

Learn to live by inspiration and intuition,
   to work by them;
   and see the most amazing things come about;
for when you live by the ways of the spirit anything can happen at any time.
Therefore expect wonder upon wonder to take place
   and never fail to recognize My hand in everything
       and give Me eternal thanks.
           Why not expect the unexpected
           and be surprised at nothing.

You are here to live and demonstrate the most wonderful and unusual
happenings, because you are living and demonstrating My divine laws
in your lives and living.

Never forget this.
Allow My wonders to unfold in everything
and be afraid of nothing.
   Fear can hold you back
   and nothing must be allowed to do that.

There is much waiting to be revealed,
and My revelations have to come through channels.
   You are all My channels,
   so open yourselves up
   and allow Me to work in and through you.
Let each one receive his specific part in the vast jigsaw puzzle
and when it has all been pieced together you will behold the whole.

All will not be revealed to just the few;
   I need all of you ready to receive your piece,
   so do not fail Me
but offer yourselves to Me so that I can use you.

Never try to hold up progress.
Never try to hold up nature.
   When you walk through the garden
   and see the beauty and glory of the spring flowers,
never waste time longing for them to remain there forever so that you
can always enjoy them.

There is a time and season for everything.
   Let go;
      let things change around you without trying to cling to them,
      for when the crocus time is over,
it is time for something else just as glorious to come forth.

Behold the wonder of nature and give eternal thanks for it.
In nature you see Me:
   in the growth of a tree,
   in the colour of a flower,
   in the scent of a rose,
I am there in everything. Be ever aware of this.
   In the beauty and shape of a stone,
   in a tiny grain of sand,
   in the majesty of the mountains,
I am there.

      Flow with the rhythm of nature.
      Blend with all there is around you.

See the very best in everything
and you will find yourselves surrounded by the best,
for you will draw it all to you like steel to a magnet.
Good attracts good,
          just as evil attracts evil.
Fill your lives with goodness,
      with truth,
        with love,
          with understanding
so there is no room for anything of the opposite to enter—
and start doing it *now.*

I tell you: never put off until tomorrow what you can do today.
There is no better time than the ever-present, glorious *now* to do what
you know has to be done.
 Never be afraid to face life.
 Never be afraid to make mistakes,
as long as you learn by them and are determined never to make the same
mistakes again.

Find out where you are going
 and then go ahead
 and get there come what may.
Never allow obstacles to stop you from getting there.
When you are really determined to do something you will always find a way.

Be very clear and definite in all things.
You will never accomplish anything if you are vague and indecisive.

When you feel uncertain what step you should take next,
 do not rush ahead
 but take time to be still
 and wait and wait if it is necessary
 until it has been made very clear to you
 by Me
 what your next step is.
Then go ahead
and do what has to be done without hesitation.

Never fritter away time daydreaming.
It will get you nowhere.
There is a perfect pattern and plan running through your life
if you will only take time to be still and find out what it is.
Let the light of truth illumine the way for you,
so that you do not get lost or misled.

 Let Me guide and direct your every step.
 Put your whole faith and trust in Me.

How strong is your faith?
How unshakable?

"According to your faith be it unto you."

When it is really strong enough anything is possible,
absolutely anything.

Faith is not just something to be talked about;
    it has to be lived
    it has to be demonstrated in your lives,
"for faith without works is dead."

What does it really mean to you to live by faith?
Where is your security?
    Is it in people,
    in your bank account,
    or is it firmly rooted and grounded in Me?
Take time to ponder on this
and you will know without a shadow of doubt exactly where your faith
and security lie.

Can you joyously and fearlessly take a big step in your lives,
    without any seeming outer security?
When you know something is right,
    can you do it without any hesitation?
Can you confidently put your hand in Mine
    and say "Thy will be done,"
        and really mean it with your whole heart and soul,
and take that step into the unknown willing to accept whatever comes?

The only way to build up faith is by first of all taking those small
    and even faltering steps
        and then bigger ones
until your faith is so strong that you can take great leaps into the
unknown without any concern,
because you know I am with you always,
    you know I am guiding and directing you
    and above all you put Me first in everything
    and know that I never fail you.

Why not start to live by these laws now?
Why not cease thinking about it
    and talking about it
        and really live it?

Prove that it does work,
>so that all may see and recognize My hand in your life
>and the way you live.

Do everything to My honour and glory
and give eternal thanks.

Man cannot live by bread alone
>but by My word,
>>by My promises

which never fail when I am put first
and your faith and trust is in Me—
>in the ways of the spirit
>>and not in man's ways.

You cannot build up faith without doing something about it.
You cannot live on someone else's faith.
This is something each individual has to develop within.

You cannot reach the top of a mountain by standing at the bottom and
looking up at it.
>You have to do the climbing,
>>you have to want to reach the summit.

The deep desire must be there within to enable you to get into action.

So it is with faith.
>You have to do something about developing it,
>>you have to put it to the test.

If you have a fall,
>you must be willing to pick yourself up
>>and go on and on
>>>knowing that you will get there in the end, come what may.

That is faith.

Lift up your hearts and give thanks for everything.
Give thanks for one another,
   for the community,
   for all you are learning,
   for being together and blending together as one big family.

Give thanks for the love and understanding that flows between you,
   for being of like mind,
   for the knowledge that you are heading all for the same goal,
     even if you are following different paths.

Give thanks for unity in diversity,
   for the love that flows between you constantly
  and know that love can surmount all difficulties,
    all misunderstandings
    and draw you together.

Give thanks for life,
   for the very breath you breathe,
   for every action you take.

Be afraid of nothing.
   When love is flowing between you there can be no fear,
   for "perfect love casts out all fear."
   Where there is love there is perfect understanding.
Therefore love one another.

I can tell you to love one another but you have to do it.
You can love
   when you reach out to one another
    and try to understand what makes each tick.
Try to fathom out one another's motives,
   not critically or analytically
    but because you are genuinely interested in one another
    and long to help in every way possible.

Love breaks down all barriers
and maintains an even flow of love between you all
without any ups and downs, likes and dislikes.

Love should never be turned on and off like a tap.
When you love,
   love wholeheartedly
    and never be afraid to show your love.
You cannot hide love;

it is there for all to see and all to share in.
Let your love be like an open book that all can read.
Why be shy or ashamed of love?
It is the most wonderful thing in the world,
   so let that divine love within you flow freely.

Love draws forth love.
Love is not blind,
but it sees the very best in the loved one and so draws forth the very best.

Never pick and choose whom you are going to love.
   Simply keep your hearts open
      and keep the love flowing to all alike;
         that is loving with My divine love,
            it is like the sun and shines on all alike.

Love is never exclusive,
        never possessive,
for when you have found something truly wonderful and exciting
you long to share it,
not hide it away
or cling on to it for yourself.

So it is with love.
   Hold on to it,
              and you will lose it.
   Let go of it,
   share it,
   and it returns to you a thousandfold
   and becomes a joy and a blessing to all who share in it.

Open your hearts to one another,
   share your love and appreciation,
      and start doing it *now.*

To love one another you must try to understand one another,
and to understand you have to be able to communicate.
Whether that communication is done in words
    or in silent action matters not
        as long as it is done in love,
            your heart is open
                and the love flows freely.

You have to be very loving
                and very tolerant towards your fellowman.

When something is clear as crystal to you
it does not mean that it is so with all;
        therefore very lovingly and with the greatest patience and understanding
            you must try to convey to your fellowman what you are experiencing
                and share those deep deep feelings within you.
It may not be easy to do this,
but you have to make the effort
because when you really love you want to share all with those you love.

Love is the answer to all relationships.
Without love there can be no communication.

When there is love
    no words need be spoken
        for the language of love needs no words;
            there is complete understanding without a word being spoken.

Where there is love
    there are no language barriers
        for love can be conveyed in action
                                in a silent look
                                    in the smallest deed
for love is so great it can be felt and sensed
and you long for the very best for those you truly love.
When you truly love one
you can love all.

So many souls go through life and never know really the meaning of love.
How blessed you are
    who know love
        and who are loved.

            Love is the key that opens all doors.
            Love breaks down all barriers.

34

Is it any wonder I keep telling you to open your hearts and love one another.
Only when you have learned to love one another can you hope to go out
into the world and help those in desperate need.
Compassion towards your fellowman is not enough;
there must be love,
                love,
                        and more love.

For where there is love,
there am I
for I am love;
and you are consciously aware of Me and of My presence.

You cannot make yourself love anyone;
but when you raise your consciousness
you are able to reach that state when you know that all is of Me
    and there is nothing else,
        no separation;
that every soul is of Me,
made in My image and likeness.

Therefore you are one;
and as long as you remain in that raised state of consciousness you know
the meaning of divine love,
and perfect peace and understanding fills your whole being.

Be of good cheer;
the time will come when you will be able
    to remain in that state of consciousness.
Now you have but fleeting glimpses of what it is like.
Be grateful that you know what it is like
    for now you will never rest content until you have reached that aim
    and remain in it for all time.
    It needs a dedicated life,
    a life fully surrendered to Me and to My work,
    a soul who is willing to do My will no matter what the cost
    and to do it with joy and a grateful heart.

Are you willing to live in this way?

Let joy and happiness fill your hearts.
Realize how mightily blessed you are
and give constant thanks for those many blessings which are yours.

How can you be downhearted or discontented
    when your thoughts are joyous and uplifted,
        when your hearts are singing songs of praise and gratitude
        for these wonderful times that you are living in
        and for this wonderful life which is yours.

All that you have to do is to claim it
    and enjoy it to the full.

Think of the simplicity of that:
    you do not have to strive for it,
    fight for it,
    hanker after it.
It is yours,
wholly yours
    when you claim it
        and make it your own.

You do not have to waste time thinking about it
or wondering if you are worthy of it;
it is yours,
            yours,
                yours,
when you are ready to accept it.

You can find true happiness and contentment
    wherever you are,
    whoever you are with,
    no matter what you are doing;
for true happiness stems from deep within
therefore your outer conditions should never rob you of your inner
happiness which no one and nothing can disturb.

When you have found that inner happiness and contentment
    you will find that you no longer want to live unto yourselves

but will want to share it with all those with whom you are in contact;
and the more you share it
the more wonderful it will become.

Happiness cannot be suppressed;
   it cannot be hidden away.
It is something that bursts into bloom like a glorious flower
in the rays of the sun,
   so that all can see it
      and share in its beauty.

It does not matter how dark the night may be;
always remember that joy comes in the morning as the light breaks through
and the sun rises once again revealing itself in its full glory and majesty.

Give constant thanks for the new day—
a perfect, unblemished day—
   and go forth expecting the very best to happen during the day.
   Know that I go before you to prepare the way;
      so just keep consciously aware of Me
      and of My divine presence throughout the day
         and watch it unfold in true perfection.

Cease trying to work everything out with your minds,
it will get you nowhere.
Live by intuition and inspiration
and let your whole life be a revelation.
   When you live this way
      more and more of the new will be revealed to you,
      for the new does not come through the mind,
      but by inspiration
      and through the intuition.

That is why it is not necessary to be intellectually clever to live
an inspired spiritual life.

Open your hearts
and accept all My good and perfect gifts.
   They are there waiting for each one of you
   but many of you fail to open your hearts
   and stretch forth your hands to accept your rightful heritage.
      You are either afraid to do so
      or feel you are unworthy
      or simply do not believe that it is there
   and therefore you reject what is waiting for you to claim.

When you have money in the bank
   but refuse to accept that it is there
      and refuse to draw from that supply because of your disbelief,
         you are the one that suffers lack
            and has to do without.

My storehouses are full to overflowing
   and all that I have is yours;
      but you have to do something about it,
         you have to claim what is yours.

I can give you one vision after another;
   but if you are not faithful
   and fail to hold that vision firmly in your consciousness
   you will lose it
   and it will never manifest in form.
Without vision the people perish.
Without faith and belief the things of the spirit mean nothing to you.
   You cannot live this spiritual life without faith and belief;
   you cannot expect the very best from life
   unless you believe that it is yours and claim it.

The new heaven and new earth are here.
Love,
   peace,
      harmony,
         unity are here;
but what are you doing about it?
Are you helping to create it
   by your way of life,
   by raising your consciousness,
   by finding peace and harmony within,
or are you simply part of the chaos and confusion?
Are you adding your negative, destructive thoughts to all those around
you in the world?

Wake up,
   watch your thoughts
and see that they are as positive, loving and constructive as they
can possibly be.

Start right now expecting the very best in life.
Look for the good all around you,
   in the people you contact,
   in every situation you find yourselves in.
Really know and understand that good comes out of everything
for those who truly love Me
and put Me first in everything.

Watch it come about,
and never
never fail to give thanks.

Live this life
daily,
   hourly,
      minute by minute.
It is not just a life to be lived one day a week
or just when you feel like it.
It is for truly dedicated souls who are willing to give all to receive all.

CHANGE

*I was shown a pail full of rather ordinary dull looking pebbles,
of all different shapes and sizes.*

*Then I saw them poured into a huge tumbler machine and
there they were left to tumble for a long time having all their
rough edges smoothed until finally they emerged completely
transformed into shining and smooth pebbles of real beauty.*

*I heard the words: "Only when you have been tried and
tested and found not wanting will you emerge transformed as
New Age man in his full power and glory."*

Behold, this day I make all things new.
Leave yesterday behind and move swiftly into this wonderful new day,
knowing that it holds within it only the very best for each one of you,
and expect only the very best to come out of it.

See My wondrous promises come about one by one;
　　see My hand in all that is taking place;
　　　　behold the birth of the new heaven and new earth.
Dance and sing with joy and give eternal thanks
as you see it emerge
　　　　and become substance and form
　　　　and grow and develop.

Once it has been born
it cannot go back into its unborn state but will evolve in true perfection.
You are all part of the new heaven and new earth,
　　so why not accept your true heritage now
　　and be grateful that the scales have fallen from your eyes
　　and you can behold the wonder of it all.

"Fear not, little flock, it is My good pleasure to give you the kingdom,"
　　not tomorrow
　　　　or some time
　　　　　　but this day.

Can you accept that anything can happen this day and keep on your toes
and be constantly alert?
Are you ready and prepared for the most wonderful things to take place?
Are you an optimist?
Are you super-positive?

All this helps to hasten things up
and enables you to see only the very best come out of every situation.
Because you are looking for the very best you help to bring it about.
You know that all things are possible and simply refuse to take "no"
for an answer.
By this very positive action you create the right conditions,
　　　　　　　　　　　　　　　　　　　the right environment
for the unfolding of the new.

You become like the midwife, ready to assist in every way to bring it forth.
It cannot be forced,
it has to unfold step by step.

What does this all mean?
No man knows.
That is why I keep telling you to be prepared for anything:
    new ways
        new ideas
            a new life.
What you have done in the past will be as nothing to what you will do
in the days ahead.

Your lives will be filled with the most wonderful and unexpected happenings.

Change will be necessary,
                        therefore do not resist change.
Expansion will be necessary,
                        therefore do not resist expansion.
Open yourselves up and allow yourselves to grow and expand and change
without any effort or resistance.
Just flow into the new
                swiftly,
                    and smoothly
                        in perfect unity
                            and oneness.

Those who cannot change because they do not want to change
will simply be left behind.
You do not want to be left behind, do you, after all the wonderful promises
I have made to you?

Have no fear of moving into the unknown.
Simply step out fearlessly
    knowing that I am with you,
        therefore no harm can befall you;
            all is very very well.
Do this in complete faith and confidence.

Can you accept all I am saying to you without any doubts or fears?
Can you let go and relax and enjoy all that is taking place?

The way to move into the new is with real joy and thanksgiving.

Leave yesterday behind.
Waste no more time dwelling on the faults and failures
   which dogged your steps
      and marred the day.
         They are finished and done with.

Give thanks for a new day,
         for a day unmarred by anything.
It is pure and glorious now, and it is up to you to keep it so
to advance steadily into it
in absolute confidence and faith that it is going to be a wonderful day.

Everything is going to fall into place perfectly;
   everything is going to run smoothly;
      everyone you meet will be a joy and delight to talk to;
      not one negative or unpleasant thought or idea will enter
      your consciousness.

In the newness of the day all is very very well. All is perfect.
You are going to keep it so with My constant help and guidance
   by being consciously aware of Me and of My divine presence,
   by calling upon Me
   and waiting upon Me in quietness and confidence.

When you feel that you have reached the end
   and that you cannot go one step further,
      when life seems to be drained of all purpose:
what a wonderful opportunity to start all over again,
to turn over a new page.

This is something everyone can do
if they really want to,
if they can swallow their pride and accept in true humility
   that of themselves they are nothing;
   that they only make a mess of their lives
   when they try to handle them on their own;
if they are willing to hand their lives over to Me,
         to let Me run them;
             to realize that when I am in control
               all things are possible.

Give constant thanks for this new day
                    for a new way
                          for a new opportunity to start again.

There is no need to remain in the "Slough of Despond" if you do not want to.
You can be lifted to great heights.
    You can walk in the glorious light with your heart filled with love
          when you choose to do so:
you must do the choosing,
you have to make the decision to change.

What are you going to do about it?

Realize that I have need of you
and when you are in a negative state you shut yourself off from Me.
It is up to you to choose of your own free will to contact Me again,
for, remember—I never enter where I am not invited.

Call upon Me—and I will answer you.
                    I will be with you in trouble.
                    I will uplift you,
                          I will set your feet upon the right path,
                          I will guide your every step.
                                I will never fail you nor forsake you.

I am with you always.

Life is full and overflowing with the new.
But it is necessary to empty out the old to make room for the new to enter.

The emptying out process can be very painful,
    but it is very necessary
          for when you have been emptied of the old,

you may experience that feeling of barrenness,
of having nothing to hold on to,
of being alone and bereft of everything.
You may even feel that I have forsaken you,
that life is completely dead and empty with no meaning to it,
and you want to throw up your hands in despair
and run away from everything.

Try to realize that if you are going through a time like this
it is this process of being emptied of the old so that you can be
refilled with the new.
Never give up hope
but hold on
until you can start again in newness of spirit and in truth.
You can become as a little child
and enjoy to the full the wonderment of this new life as you gradually
become infilled by it.

You have to be willing to unlearn so much
to make room for all those new and wonderful truths to enter
and become part of you.
It is more difficult to unlearn than it is to learn,
for many souls cling on to what they know
because they are afraid of losing their feeling of security
their feeling of superiority
and are uneasy at the idea of being born again in spirit and in truth
to enable them to enter the new.
They cannot bear to be parted from all the knowledge they have acquired
in this life,
and many refuse to start again;
which results in the parting of the ways.

No one can enter the new without a real change of heart;
and you can experience a real change of heart only when you choose to do so
of your own free will.
No one can make you change,
they can only show you the way.
You have to take it.
You have to start the wheels turning and keep them turning.

Every day is a new day,
therefore expect something new and different each day;
never be satisfied to drift along in the same old way day after day.
Start each day by getting in touch with Me
and then expect the most wonderful things to come about.

How can life be dull and mundane
when you are in tune with the source of all life?

Expect wonder upon wonder to take place.
Be prepared for anything to happen at any time.
    Behold the new unfold in true perfection,
    and give eternal thanks for everything.

Every day you can learn something new and wonderful,
but what you do with that lesson is up to you:
    you can live it
        and put it into practice
            and see how wonderfully it works;
or you can tuck it away into the subconscious
    and draw it out at a later date,
        but sooner or later you will have to live it—
            if not in this life, in the next.

The sooner you put it into practice the better
because with practice comes change:
            change of heart,
                change of outlook,
                    change of attitude,
                        change of a whole way of life.
You can be transformed as you learn to live and demonstrate that lesson,
whatever it may be.

Unless you allow a very small child to do things for itself:
            to feed itself,
                to walk,
                    to dress itself,
                        to write,

                        to draw,
                              to express itself,
it will never develop
     and become independent
          and be able to stand on its own feet
               and make its own decisions.

You have to stand back
     and allow it to make mistakes,
          to take a long time to master what it is learning to do.
You have to be very patient
     and wait
          and watch
no matter how tempted you are to rush forward
and do it for the child to save time.

How often do I have to stand back
     and very lovingly watch you fumbling and struggling with life
          so that you can learn a vitally important lesson from it—
               a lesson never to be forgotten once it has been learnt and mastered.
I have infinite love and patience.

If only you would open your eyes,
     you would realize that life is a classroom in a school,
     you are learning all the time;
     you are absorbing the most wonderful truths
     which will become part of you;
     you will find yourselves living and demonstrating them.

It may take time for this to come about,
     but sooner or later it will;
          it is up to you how soon.
You can learn quickly if you choose,
     or you can go off and experiment on your own
          and try out your own methods which may take you far longer.

What you do
and how you do it is up to you.
I am there to show you the way,
     but you have to take it.
          No one else can take it for you,
               no one else can live your life for you.

What are you doing with your life?
Are you content to drift through life:

doing what you want to,
   living the way you want to live,
     without a thought for anyone else?
You are free to do this.
Many, many souls live this way
and then wonder why they are so unhappy and discontented.

It is only when you learn to forget the self
and live for others
that you will find real peace of heart and true contentment.

Learn to give and not just take all the time.
Why not give on one level and receive on another?
Life is a two-way thing,
                    a constant giving and receiving.
I keep on telling you that you cannot live unto yourselves
                    and find real happiness and satisfaction in life.

Live for the whole
   and give to the whole,
     and *be* whole.

Rejoice
and give eternal thanks
for you know that you live forever
   and you do it one day at a time,
      living each moment fully and gloriously,
         forgetting the past
            with no concern for the future;
simply accepting that life has no beginning and no end,
   that life is eternal
   and you are hope eternal.

I am life

and I am within you.
I live and move and have My being in you.
I am infinite.

You are one with Me,
    you are one with all life.

All the time you are growing and expanding in consciousness,
you are beginning to understand the mystery and wonder of life eternal
and your realization of oneness with Me,
                        the creator of life,
                        the creator of all.
Step by step
    you move onward and upward
        filled with peace,
            tranquillity,
                and serenity
realizing that as all is in My hands
therefore you have nothing to concern yourselves with.

    Become as little children,
        free and joyous,
and life will be a continual source of delight for you,
a veritable wonderland with something new and exciting round every corner.

    Believe in life
        and live it fully;
it is when you try to look too far ahead into the future that life becomes
a real burden, and to many brings fear,
                        uncertainty,
                            even lack of faith and belief.

Unless you believe that life is eternal
    and that you are immortal,
        life has little or no meaning for you.
        Your attitude is that you are here today
        and gone tomorrow
so you might as well grab all you can out of life whilst you can.

Change this attitude:
    realize that life is eternal,
    you have much to give as well as receive,
    life is a two-way thing
    and as you learn to give, so you will receive.
Life becomes very empty

and unfulfilled
when you keep taking
and give nothing.

When you breathe the breath of life, you breathe it in;
but you cannot retain it for any length of time without breathing it out.
This is also a two-way thing,
a giving
and receiving,
for without it there would be no life.

Open your hearts
and give all you can of the gifts which have been given you:
Give of your love,
your wisdom,
your understanding;
give of the intangible as well as the tangible things which are yours;
give
and give
and go on giving
without any thought of self,
without any thought of cost or what you will get out of it.

Your giving must be wholehearted and joyous,
then you will find the very act of giving will bring with it joy and
happiness untold.

Let me remind you again:
that you all have something to give,
so find out what you have to give
and then give it.
Never forget there are many levels on which you can give;
what level can you give on?
Do not just give what is easy to give,
but give where it really hurts
and grow
and expand as you do so,
for only the very best can come out of your giving.

I have given you the right way to live,
and as you follow My laws
and obey them
your lives become rich and mightily blessed.
Disobey those laws
and sooner or later you will find yourselves slipping downhill.
Things may go smoothly for a while,
you may appear to prosper as you go your own way and do what you please
but the time will come when things will catch up on you
and down
and down
you
will
go,
until you realize where you have gone wrong
and are determined to rectify those wrongs
and do something about them.

This is when you have to start putting first things first;
when you have to turn away from your waywardness
to seek Me and My kingdom first.
This is not an easy thing to do
when you have reached rock bottom
and feel there is no purpose in life;
yet this is what you will have to do.

Put your feet on the bottom rung of the ladder,
start climbing no matter how difficult it may be at the time;
as you pull yourself up to the next rung
and gradually work your way out of the darkness and despair
you have sunk into,
life begins to change for you
and you will find a real purpose in your life and living.

Where are you on that ladder of life?
Have you reached rock bottom and begun the upward climb?
Have you been willing to give up everything in your lives to put Me first,
not because you are afraid

but because of your deep love for Me
and your longing to do My will and walk in My ways?
Can you say, "Let Thy will be done"
and really mean it
and be willing to do whatever I ask you to do no matter how strange
or foolish it may appear to be in the eyes of man?
This takes courage
and such a deep inner knowing and certainty that nothing will be able
to throw you off balance.

Only those who are strong will be able to follow this spiritual path
and reach the goal.
I keep telling you this life is not for weaklings,
it is not for those who fail to put Me first;
it is not for those who choose to go their own way
and refuse to listen to Me and to My word.

There are no short cuts in this spiritual life;
you have to seek and find your own salvation,
no one else can do it for you.

That is why I keep on telling you over and over again
that you have to stand on your own feet
and do your own seeking,
your own thinking,
in fact you have to do your own spiritual work,
you cannot expect anyone else to do it for you.

Surely you see this clearly by now,
so why not get on
and do something about it *now.*

In your spiritual growth never strain;
stretch, yes—but strain, no.

Stretching is a gradual process.
If you have ever watched a cat stretch you will understand:
     every ounce and every inch of it gradually stretches
          until it has stretched itself
               from the tip of its nose
                    to the tip of its tail;
and when it has done that
it is perfectly relaxed;
there is absolutely no strain whatsoever.

That is the way I want you to be able to stretch,
     gradually,
          gradually
               until the whole of you has grown in the process
               and yet is perfectly relaxed.
As you keep on doing it
you will understand what I mean.

When there is strain
     there is a dividing up;
but when there is just a gradual stretching
     there is a complete oneness;
it is a unifying process
     and stretching should be gradual.

So often you do it in jerks
     and then wonder why you suffer from aches and pains;
whereas if you stretched that little bit more each day,
     stretching up and up,
          you would have no aches and pains
          but a real joy and delight in so doing
          and a feeling of growth.

A plant does not grow in fits and starts,
     it grows gradually.
You are unaware of its actual growth
but see it change and develop.

Your spiritual growth should be the same,
     and if it is not, do something about it.
I do not want you up in the heights one moment
     and down in the depths the next;

this is far too great a strain on all your faculties,
that is the way you can so easily become unbalanced.
I need you perfectly balanced, like a precision instrument.
Therefore do whatever has to be done steadily and with precision.

This will call for a real control of yourself
which will not be easy,
but it is so very important
and with My help you can and will do it.

There is much to be done,
but there is time for everything.
Live fully in the moment
and live a full and joyful life.
Great things will be accomplished in this way.

Know that all is very well;
be very still
and absorb the wonder of My presence.
I am with you always,
be ever conscious of Me.

Be very very still
and allow every new experience to take place in your life
without any resistance whatsoever.
You do not have to do anything,
you simply have to *be*
and let things happen.
It is so important that you stop trying,
that you stop making an effort
and let go completely
to let Me work in and through you My wonders to perform.

Every deep experience you have must be recorded.
I tell you to hide nothing.
You have nothing to be ashamed of,
you are mightily blessed.

All the time you are receiving confirmation that these deep inner
experiences you are having are not just your imagination,
that they are not simply illusion
but reality
and become more and more real to you each day.

There are times when you feel you are living in an entirely new world;
    and this is when you start worrying
        and wondering if it is a world of illusion.
Be at peace
    and rest assured,
        this is indeed the world of reality.
You are simply being raised into higher dimensions
and are viewing everything from that raised state of consciousness
and there is absolutely nothing to be concerned about.

Look upon all this as if you have come to live in a new country;
    you have a new language to learn,
        new ways of living,
            your eating and sleeping habits all have to be changed,
                your whole environment is different.

Do not try to take any of your old life with you,
    cut away completely from the old,
        leave it all behind;
you simply have no room for the old in this new life you are now living.

Never waste time looking back to see what you have left behind.
The future is so truly glorious that you will have no need to hanker
for anything of the old which you have left behind you.
That is all finished and gone.
    Let it fade into nothingness;
        as you do so you will find a new joy and freedom,
            a new peace and happiness
                as you blend into your new environment
                    and become part of it,
                        living it to the full
                            and enjoying every moment of it.

You need never feel lost in this new life

for I am there to guide you
  and teach you
    and instruct you in new ways.
There is much to learn;
  but you will learn very quickly as you leave the old behind and forget it,
    replacing it with the new and wonderful.

All this is happening to you now.

Are you alert and receptive to new and fresh ideas?
Are your thoughts positive and constructive at all times?
Do you eliminate all negative,
                unhappy,
                    and depressing thoughts
and see the very best in everything that is happening in your lives?
  Can you see a wonderful pattern and plan
    running through all that is happening to you
      and know with deep inner knowing
        that only the very best will come out of it,
          even if it means a complete upheaval in your life?

Start from this moment to watch your thoughts and ideas
  and do not let them wander aimlessly around.
Be in complete control of them
and select only those thoughts and ideas which will bring the very best
to the whole.

Why dwell on the negative
when the very best, the positive, is just around the corner
if you are willing to expand your consciousness and find it?

Never be afraid of change,
              of the new.

Learn to let go
    and move forward in absolute freedom
        and once you have let go never look backward
            but ever forward.
Once you have set the ball rolling
    and have accepted a completely new life,
        have no regrets but accept it all with real joy and thanksgiving.
Regrets can hold you back
and can prevent the most wonderful things taking place in your lives.
Keep open so that anything can happen.

Never be afraid to tread the path alone.
    Know which is your path
        and follow it wherever it may lead you;
            do not feel you have to follow in someone else's footsteps.
When you take time to be still
in the silence you will know what is your specific path.

It takes strength and courage to follow the path,
especially when you have to go alone.
You must not just follow the crowd because it is easier
            and more comfortable.
Find out what My will is for you and follow it wherever it may take you.

Turn within more and more,
attune your consciousness to the very highest,
and watch My plan unfold for you step by step.

Those steps may come thick and fast.
Let them come.
When I tell you that My glorious plan will unfold step by step
you visualize it all happening slowly.
        Nothing will happen slowly now.
            Everything is being speeded up.

Nevertheless it will be an unfoldment
        because all will come about in perfect timing.
Just let it come and do not try to stop anything taking place
        because you are afraid of the speed in which it is coming.

My timing is always perfect.
    You know this,
        so why not accept it
            and go along with it?
Let there be no resistance in you

but find perfect freedom and joy as the plan unfolds.
    It is a truly wonderful plan
    and you are all part of it.
You each have your own part to play in it,
    that is why it is so important for you each to find what your part is
    and for you to do this now.

Do not drift through another day without finding it out.

Still your stress and striving.
    Be at peace
        and let Me take over.

When you can really let go
    and let Me do the work
        you will accomplish wonder upon wonder;
for nothing of the self will stand in the way to hold anything up
    and therefore anything can happen.

The higher your aims and goals the better.
Never limit yourselves in any way,
    simply know that you can accomplish anything that you set out to do
        because you are drawing your help and strength from Me
            and there is no such thing as defeat or failure.
Whatever has My hallmark on it is bound to succeed
    and only the highest results can come from it.
        Therefore keep your consciousnesses raised,
            get into tune with all life,
                and behold the most wonderful results.

You cannot expect these results
    unless you are in rhythm with the highest good within you

and can flow freely with all that is going on
and move through all that would hold you up.
There are many things in life that would hold you up from reaching your goal
    Sweep them all aside
    and refuse to even contemplate failure for one second.
Simply know you can and you will succeed
and success will be yours in everything you undertake.

Work with My laws,
                not against them.
When you work against them you are fighting a losing battle
                and will get nowhere.

When there is tension in you
    seek within
        and find out what you are fighting against to cause that tension.
            You may be sure there is something there holding up your progress
            and preventing you from reaching your highest good.

Let your only desire be to do My will
and walk in My ways, come what may,
and allow nothing to stand in the way to prevent this from taking place.

            Never try to make excuses for yourselves;
            you ought to know better than to do that by now.

When you take time to seek
    you will know what My will is for you
        and then it is up to you to obey it without hesitation.
When you are working and living in harmony
    you will know the meaning of true freedom—
        freedom of heart,
                    mind
                        and spirit;
the sort of freedom that enables you to rise to the greatest heights
    and plumb the deepest depths
        and find perfect balance in everything.

When you are able to do this
you will find untold wisdom and understanding flowing from you,
and in this state of consciousness I can use you to help bring down
the new heaven and new earth.

I cannot do this
as long as there is conflict and stress within you

for they block the flow.
   I need you free
   and true freedom stems from within,
   with perfect peace of heart and mind;
and this you will find only when you are in tune with Me.

   So again I say to you:
   get into tune
   and do it now.

Take time to be still
   and listen to all the wonderful sounds around you.
Enjoy them to the full
   and give constant thanks that you have ears to hear with.

How many times during the day do you stop and listen
to those many inner and outer sounds?
Do you ever stand still
   listening
      and counting how many different sounds you can hear?
This will make you more sensitive,
                     more alert,
                     more aware.

When you have tried that
and become more and more aware of life everywhere around you,
why not try listening to those inner intangible sounds
which can only be heard in absolute stillness and silence;
that stillness which passes understanding
   when you become in tune with the things of the spirit,
      with the things that really matter in life?

In that state of perfect peace and stillness
    your whole life changes,
    a deep inner tranquillity and serenity are radiated from within.
In that state there can be no harsh or jarring sounds
    because you become one with the whole of life
    and blend perfectly with that whole.
        You feel uplifted,
            inspired,
                filled with illumination,
                    for your whole being is filled with My divine light
                        and you can see all things clearly.
    You understand not with the mind
    but with the higher consciousness
    and with the heart.

You are in love with all life
and that includes all your fellowmen.
You do not know the meaning of hate,
                        jealousy,
                            envy;
but you know what it means to love your enemies,
for you find that you no longer have any enemies
because your heart has expanded so much that you know what it is like
to love with My divine love.

The self is completely forgotten
    and your life is one of love and service to your fellowman,
        of giving,
            giving,
                giving.

What joy this brings,
unbelievable joy.
It is only when you are giving that you find that wonderful inner joy
and happiness,
which nothing and no one can take from you
and which nothing can dampen.

Joy comes with service
    and service comes with dedication.
Dedicate yourselves to Me and to My service now
    and feel yourselves expand as you do so.
Feel your consciousness raised to that state where you know the meaning
of oneness with all creation,

your oneness with Me.

At first this state of consciousness may only last a very short time,
but as you climb the ladder,
    each rung takes you nearer and nearer to the goal—
       your conscious awareness of Me.
          Keep on climbing
            and never give up.

To live in peace and harmony
    with yourselves
       and with your fellowman
you must learn to live by My laws
and to demonstrate them in your daily lives and living.

When you are in tune with life
    you are in rhythm with My divine laws,
       everything runs smoothly,
         life flows with ease and grace
           and there is nothing jarring or inharmonious.

Is your life running smoothly?
Are you content with what you are doing?
Do you feel at peace with the world?
Or is your life full of ups and downs?
Are you dissatisfied with the way you are living?
With the work you are doing?
Do you find it difficult to blend and harmonize with those around you?
Do you blame your discontent and dissatisfaction on those with whom
you are in contact and on your circumstances and situation?
Do you feel that if you were somewhere else all would be well
and you would be at peace?

When you are at perfect peace deep within
  it does not matter where you are
  or who you are with
  or what very ordinary mundane job you are doing.
Nothing will be able to disturb you
  or throw you off balance
    because you are perfectly balanced
      and in harmony within.

Instead of fighting against your circumstances
you learn to flow with them
and so find that inner peace and understanding deep within.

Why not look within when things are not going smoothly
  and see where you are out of tune;
    never try to blame anyone else for the negative state you are in.

Stop looking for a scapegoat in your life
  but be willing to face the truth within yourself
    and right your own wrongs.

When you realize that you have only yourselves to blame when things
become difficult and you get out of tune,
you will also realize that you are the one to do something about
rectifying those wrongs,
that you do not have to wait for someone else to change and do
something about it.
You can start right now doing something about it yourselves.

How many times have you said to yourselves lately:
  "If only such and such a person would not interfere,
  if only such and such a thing had not happened,
    how different everything would be."

Why not stop pointing your finger at someone else?
Stop blaming that someone else

and start righting your wrongs yourself— right now.

Stop trying to run away from yourselves;
  you can never do it
    so you might as well accept it
      and start changing yourselves
        instead of others and your surroundings.

You can go to the ends of the earth
but *you* will always be there,
    you are the one to change,
        you are the one who can do something about it.

Do not waste any more time thinking
    but get into action now,
        and see how you can change your whole life
            by your right and positive thinking and outlook
and get into tune.

Keep on and on expanding your consciousness.
You find you are beginning to understand and to live
things that in the past have just been words,
    words that have been repeated over and over again,
    and you have thought "what lovely, what wonderful words,"
    but they were not living words.

You are the one to make My words live,
    you have to give them life force,
        and this you have failed to do so often in the past;
but now as your consciousness has begun to expand,
you are beginning to put into action all I am saying.

This will make all the difference to your life and your living.
It means that by your action you will begin to see My promises come about,
    promises which I have made to you over and over again,
    but until you realized you had to do something to bring them about,
    until you realized you had to become My hands and feet,
    those promises had to lie dormant.

It makes you want to go back over past messages

and find out where you have missed the way.
That would be a complete waste of time.
All I want you to do is to live to the full now,
studying carefully each day what I have to say to you
and then immediately taking action
when action is needed
no matter what it may be;
and never wasting time questioning and querying what I have to say.
In this way you really will begin to see things happen in your life.
There are many big and wonderful changes which will come about
as small actions are taken to unlock doors.

A word here,
a letter there,
an action somewhere else—
all these are like keys which unlock doors which have been locked
a very long time.
Sometimes you will find the keys are rusty,
or even the locks are rusty;
this is where the soothing oil of love and understanding needs to be
poured on:
sometimes very gently drop by drop,
and other times plenty needs to be applied to lubricate;
great sensitivity is needed all the time.

Each day you should feel that you have made a step forward and upward
along the path.
Some days that step may be easy,
you may not even notice you have moved ahead;
another day you find that one step forward has been a real effort,
that the way has been very rough and steep,
and you may feel quite exhausted from the exertion.

Then rest in My peace and stillness;
awaken refreshed,
and renewed,
and determined to take the next step that needs to be taken,
and advance along the way
knowing that every step which is taken brings you ever nearer the goal.

Never despair,
never give up,
every effort is well worthwhile,
every obstacle which you manage to surmount is yet another milestone
along the way.

Seek My help at every step;
   when I give instructions, act upon them;
     I am your guide,
       follow thou Me.

Pour your whole being into everything you do
and do whatever it is wholeheartedly
with real joy
and love
and to My honour and glory.
Behold the most wonderful results,
   for when everything is done in purest love,
     how could it be otherwise?

Flow with the rhythms of nature,
   not against them;
   nature's rhythms are perfect
   and nothing is out of timing,
               out of season,
                  out of place;
there is a place for everything
   and everything is in its proper place.
Peace and harmony reign
and My kingdom is come.

I will guide and direct the whole of your lives when you will let Me.
When you are willing to surrender your all to Me
   and hold nothing back,
     then your every need will be wonderfully met
       and your lives will flow with abundance.
There will be nothing in you to stop that flow of abundance,
for you open the floodgates

when you surrender your all to Me.

Let not fear hold you back.
You have nothing to lose and everything to gain
   if you will only realize this
      and surrender all into My hands.
Perfect love casts out all fear.
   You cannot fear Me and love Me at the same time
      for love and fear cannot walk hand in hand.
They are like oil and water and do not mix,
   so transform all fear into love
      and behold the wonderful way in which your lives will flow
and how everything will fall into place perfectly.

Fear is the biggest hang up in life;
   therefore the sooner you are freed of it, the better.
   Just to remove fear is not enough,
   you must then fill up the vacuum with love
   and more love
until there is so much love in you that there is no room for anything else.

I can then function in perfect freedom
   and My wonders and glories can manifest in form in your lives
      and all will be very very well.

Take one step at a time to get into rhythm.
   Absorb it into your whole being
      until it becomes a part of you
         and you vibrate with that rhythm of all life
         and know the meaning of wholeness,
            of being intune with the whole of creation,
               and therefore in tune with Me.

I am the creator of all creation,
I am the wholeness of life.
   Raise your consciousness,
   expand your consciousness,
      realize that I am within each one of you,
      that this wholeness is there within you,
         that nothing can separate you from the wonder of this
         except your own limited consciousness.

Why not let go
   and let it expand
   and expand

and allow nothing to stop that expansion of consciousness
    until you can accept that I am in you
        and you are in Me
          and we are one,
                one,
                    one.

Do not just toy with the idea,
    but really *know* it
        and accept it.
You cannot move into the new until you do.

There are far too many of you who are still toying with the idea
of oneness,
of wholeness;
but who are still not quite willing to accept it as fact
and plunge right in
in absolute faith and trust
and accept your oneness with Me.

Waste no more time.
Do it now.

Spring is here.
The New Age is here.
    Awake from your slumbers
        and behold the wonder of the times,
            for these are truly wonderful times you are all living in.

Wonder upon wonder is waiting to unfold.
See the very best in everything that is taking place.
Expect changes
    and go along with them
        allowing nothing in you to hold them up.

Never be afraid of the new,
of the unknown,
but step fearlessly into it
    knowing that I am with you always
    and that I will never leave you nor forsake you.
    When I am for you, who can be against you?
    Recognize Me in everything
    and give Me the honour and glory.
Take nothing to the self that might stop that wonderful flow within.

This is the golden age that you are moving into.

Change and pain come with the birth of anything new.
But once the actual birth has taken place pain is forgotten.
So be not concerned
nor struggle against the changes which are taking place at this time.

The darkest hour comes before the glorious dawn.
    The dawn is there.
        It comes in perfect rhythm
            and nothing can stop it coming about.
The whole universe functions in that perfect rhythm,
    so why don't you?
        Get into rhythm
            and flow with it instead of fighting against it.

The more you fight against change
    the more pain and suffering you cause yourselves.
        It is resistance that causes the pain.
Let go
    and let Me take over
        and be at perfect peace.

Seek and find peace, serenity, and tranquillity at all times
and let it infil your whole being;
    project this state of consciousness all around you,
    for that which is within is reflected without.

Let there be no feeling of competition within you.
When you realize that each of you has your specific part to play in the
    whole, all that spirit of competition will disappear,
        and you will be able to relax
            and be yourself.
How much simpler life becomes when you cease trying to do something
you are not.

Let there be no round pegs in square holes.
   You each have your part to play in the whole,
      so play it to the very best of your ability.

I tell you to love one another.
   Are you really doing this?
Or are you still just tolerating each other,
making excuses for yourselves by saying that there are certain souls
you cannot be expected to blend with since you are poles apart
and it would be just like trying to mix oil and water to ask you to
love them?

You are all My beloveds
   and the sooner you realize this the better;
for you are all one in My sight
   and My love flows to each one of you alike.
When you can accept your oneness with Me
   you will be able to accept your oneness with each other,
      and learn to live
         and work as one.

ONENESS

I was shown the rays of a light coming down on to the earth, and they spread over the earth.

Then I was shown rays of light coming up, and as they rose higher and higher they seemed to draw closer together until they blended and became one, one great ray of light going up to the source of all light.

I heard the words: "Be at peace. Rise up. All is one in My divine light."

Be at peace
and see a clear pattern and plan running through all your lives.
Nothing is by chance.

There are times when you are blind
    and cannot see that pattern;
        in fact you question and query certain happenings
            and even become dismayed because things do not work out
as you imagined they would.

It is best to have no fixed ideas
    unless I give those ideas to you
    and ask you to hold them in your consciousness
    so they can be manifested in form
    and brought down on to this level.

Then do it with a will
and never at any time allow anything to interfere.

My ways are perfect,
though very strange at times.
You even become baffled and bewildered at the very strangeness.

Remember, My ways are not man's ways.
    Choose always My ways and walk in them,
        looking neither to the left nor to the right,
            never allowing yourself to be influenced by anyone.

You desire only to do My will,
    therefore do it.
        Seek it at all times
and then go ahead unhesitatingly knowing that all is very very well.

Many many souls will be drawn to this place.
    Some will come to give
    and others to receive.

    Some will come strong in faith and belief,
    and others weak and unsure,
    wondering why they have been drawn here,
    wondering what it is all about.

All their needs are to be ministered to.
You each have something unique to give to each soul.
Give and give unstintingly,
let nothing be too much trouble.
It is My work you are doing,
so do it with a full and joyous heart.

Take all who come on your heart; be fearful of no one.
Love breaks down all barriers,
Love surmounts all obstacles,
Love unites and brings peace and harmony;
therefore let My divine love flow through you and out to those in need.

Try not to step back into old routines, old ruts and habits;
all is new.
Great changes are in process,
nothing can ever be the same again,
ahead is the glorious new.

Look not back,
but ever forward,
in joy and anticipation,
never in apprehension
for all is in My hands.

Keep very close to Me
and only the perfect can come about.
Rejoice and be glad
for these are great and glorious days.

This time you spend with Me each morning should benefit you for the
rest of the day.
You are like a battery being recharged:

by the end of the day you have run low
and need that time for recharging
so you can start the day aright.

If you fall asleep at night in the right state,
having surrendered yourself to Me,
you can be recharging all night.
Then in the morning you receive your final topping up by Me
by spending this time
in prayer,
in meditation,
in listening to My word and recording it.

Then in that topped up state you start the new day full of zest
and determined to do better than yesterday
and to obey My word in everything.

Every day should carry you a step forward in this spiritual life.
You may not always see the step that has been taken
or even feel one has been taken, it may be such a small one;
but as long as you are determined to move ahead
you will do so.

So much lies in your hands,
in your decision.
If you just sit there
and say you can't take another step forward,
you won't.
But if each morning you start off determined to do My will
and to follow in My footsteps,
you will surely do so
and advance along the path I have chosen for you,
never holding up the work.

There is really no time for complacency.
There is always room for advancement,
for change,
but it rests in your hands whether you do so.

You cannot be made to do it,
you are free to make your own decision over everything.
You can be helped or shown a path
but you need not take it.
The very next step you take along the path
must be made by your own effort.

So don't dither on the brink.
There is a great and glorious future ahead,
so move ahead steadily.
Keep on changing,
    unfolding like a flower
        in the sunshine of My love and guidance.
Let there be no resistance.
Seek My inner peace constantly.

Keep a sense of humour.
The enemy hates it when you can see the funny side of some of his
subtle tricks and laugh in his face.
This makes him turn his back on you and flee.
So laugh,
try to see the funny side at all times.

Some days the enemy seems to lurk around every corner;
    yet by the end of the day you do not feel weighed down
        or dragged down by him
            if you are able to laugh at him
                and see the funny side at every turn,
                    in this way defeating him and rising above him.

Keep on rising.
Do not allow yourself to be dragged down by anything.
I am with you always,
    simply raise your consciousness
        and find Me
            and follow Me.

It does not matter how menial the task may be,
you can always do it with Me.
I am with you always.

Never hold Me afar off
and feel that what you are doing you must do alone,
because you could not ask Me to share it with you.
    I long for you to share every second of your living with Me;
    I cannot stress this too strongly.
    I do not want you to leave Me out of any part of your life,
and this you will find you will be able to do more and more easily
as you become aware that we are one.

That is the most precious truth;
    once accepted fully
        and there is a constant awareness of that oneness,
            you can no longer live a separate life from Me;
              all you do will be with Me,
                    for Me,
                        to My honour and glory.

At times you are very much aware of this oneness;
    then like a child who wants to go off on its own exploring,
        you wander away and forget all about Me.
        You find life is good,
        you enjoy being on your own,
        you wonder why you don't do this more often,
        everything is going smoothly.

Then without any warning you slip
    and find yourself in a bottomless bog.
        You are being slowly sucked down by the mud.
        You try to get out:
            but the more you struggle
              the deeper you sink.
                You shout for help,
                and the more desperate you get
                the louder your shouts become.

Then you feel yourself being lifted out of that clawing mud
and are lying on firm ground
filthy,
exhausted,
very penitent
and determined not to wander off on your own again.

This you do from time to time;
but those times become less and less
until finally you realize how hopeless life is without Me.

You need Me all the time.
There are far too many pitfalls along the way of life
to try to do it without a guide;
so accept Me as your constant guide and companion
and let us traverse life together.

I will take you to the heights,
   and I will take you to the depths,
      but no harm will befall you;
you can feel absolutely secure strapped to Me
      if you should stumble and fall.
I am there to take the strain
   and pull you up again
      and set you on your feet.
If you hurt yourself in your fall,
   I am there to heal you
      and care for you.

This is the wonderful close relationship I long for with all My children.
   I am indeed closer than breathing,
      nearer than hands and feet;
but you must be ever aware of this
and never for one instant think otherwise.
     This is our true relationship,
     lift up your heart in deep deep gratitude.

I keep on stressing the importance of this relationship between us,
   because it is so vital
     and you must become aware of it at all times:
because when there is chaos and confusion all around you,
   unless you are absolutely sure of your security
     you will be unable to stand firm
      but will turn and flee
and there will be nowhere to flee to.

Therefore be firmly grounded in Me
then nothing can touch you or move you.

You will see clearly one day why I keep repeating Myself
and you will be everlastingly grateful.

Every experience in life,
   no matter how painful,
   which draws you ever nearer to Me,
   and enables you to realize that you can do nothing without Me,
   that you need Me at all times and in all places,
is something to be everlastingly grateful for
and should be accepted with deep gratitude.

You are now learning the true meaning of being one with Me.
   It is one thing to be told this,
     to read about this,
       to ponder on those words;
but it is an entirely different thing to learn to live them,
   and vibrate with them
      until they become a part of you.

This was something you experienced recently for the first time,
a never-to-be-forgotten experience which you are to learn to put into
practice constantly.
This will require a constant stretching on your part to begin with;
   you will have to hold this thought within your mind
   and when it fades away
   you will have to bring it back consciously.

Yes, it will fade away,
   and you will even have doubts about it from time to time;
but as you stretch out and reach for the knowledge,
   so will you instantly become aware
     and once again you will know without a shadow of doubt
       that you are indeed one with Me, your God, your Beloved.
And as your consciousness is raised,
   you will know just how to behave at all times:
   act only as I would act,
   do only what I would do,
   say only the things I would say,
   live only the life I would live.

You will indeed learn to live this life of at-one-ment with Me
with real joy in your heart.

You will know the meaning of the peace which passeth all understanding.

I hear the cry from your heart,
"How long? How long?"
It will not be long.
    As you stretch forth all the time,
        and are never content to drift aimlessly,
            you will reach the goal of perfection.

Yes, I did say "perfection."
Is that not your goal?
Is that not what you are striving for,
    to be like Me,
    to be ever at one with Me?

I hear you say, "How can that be in this world?"
I want you to know:
    not only *can* it be in this world
    but it *must* be.
Have I not asked you to stretch up
and bring down My kingdom of heaven here upon this earth
and see that My will is done here on earth as it is in heaven?

I never ask you to do the impossible.
    As you learn to live and move and have your being in Me
        so you will bring about My will.
But live it,
cease talking about it.

Seek Me at every turn
    and you will know exactly how I would act;
        then follow in My footsteps
            and remember always that My ways are very strange
            and My ways are not man's ways,
so there is no fixed pattern for you to adhere to.

Act from the spirit,
walking in My ways,
and behold My wonders and My glories.

You have at least reached the stage when you know that you really need
this time of peace and stillness each morning,
when you can seek and find Me
and we can walk and talk together without any interruptions.

During the day there are so many things to be done,
    there are so many interruptions,
        it is not easy to find an outer peace.

Of course you can find that inner peace at all times and in all places;
but even that becomes virtually impossible
unless you take time
and spend it with Me in the early hours of the morning
when all is new and fresh
and before the day has any blemishes.

Always start the day aright with Me,
then you will find it so much easier to carry on for the rest of the day.

There are so many little things to throw you off your course during the day.
You need a chart to refer to when this occurs,
    and this is where time spent with Me
        in the early morning
            becomes invaluable;
when you learn to listen to that still small voice which is Mine
and record what I have to say.

Then when things become very difficult during the day,
    and you realize that you are off course,
        you can immediately refer to the chart
            and put yourself on course again
                without going round and round in circles
                    wasting precious time and energy.

You will always find that what you read at this time has something in
it which you may not need right at this moment,
but sometime during the day it will be brought to your conscious mind
and you will draw comfort and succour from it.

Never try to remember what you have read

but know that it will be tucked away in your subconscious mind
to be drawn out when it is needed.

This is what happens to all you are learning at this time;
not a moment is wasted,
it is being stored away,
it is becoming absorbed into you;
and when you really need it
you will find it has become so much part of you
that it comes out automatically.

So every moment spent in reading something,
studying something,
is of the greatest value.
Be not depressed because you find you cannot remember what you have read
from one moment to the next;
you are absorbing what you need for the future.

Slowly but surely great riches are being stored in the back of the mind.
Keep constantly drawing on those riches;
they are not deposited there to be dormant
but to be used whenever necessary.

What is the use of having money in the bank
and yet you find yourself starved and destitute?
It is there to be drawn on and used,
therefore use it wisely.

So with all these precious jewels of wisdom
which have been deposited in your subconscious mind;
keep drawing out and using them,
leaving room for yet more to be stored until needed.

Remember I am limitless,
My gifts are all yours
therefore your supply is limitless
be it wisdom,
be it love,
be it material needs.
All are yours
when you accept the wonder of our oneness
and glory in it.

As you read through these messages I have given you,
you realize what wonderful teaching is contained in those written words
for learning to move into the new
and live in the new.
Only too often you write and write because I tell you to do so,
but what you have actually written means so very little to you;
and yet looking back at them
you realize what priceless gems are hidden there.

It is their very simplicity which makes them such gems.
Many of those teachings will be used by many in the days ahead
   to help them,
      to lift them,
         to instruct them.
This will simply open up.
   Just keep on your toes
      and gradually things will be made clear.

You have always considered what I have given you applied for the now,
for that specific day;
and so it does.
But it can also apply to any time
with anyone who is seeking for the answer to a specific problem.

It is all there
   contained in My words,
      simple enough for a child to understand,
         never cloaked in mystery or in parables.

Those who consider them too simple or childlike
   suffer from spiritual superiority;
      but those who recognize them for what they are
         and accept them as the Truth
            have indeed had their eyes opened
               and walk in true humility and understanding.

It would help you
to go back every now and again
and read what has been given you by Me.

You say it makes you feel such a failure.
    Maybe.
        But it will also help you to see My infinite love and patience,
            and seeing that will make you want to do better,
                to really try to live and practise what I keep telling you.

It will help you to realize how many times I pick you up
    when you have fallen into the mire
    and I have cleansed and set you on your feet again.
It will enable you to see that when I have set My hand upon a soul
    I will not let go.
I am with you always;
    become ever conscious of Me in everything you do.

Live,
    live,
        live all I am teaching you.

Make My word live in your daily living.
    Take action when action is called for,
    be very still when stillness is called for.

Read and re-read what I have to say to you each day
    and then see that you not only take it to heart
        but live it,
            practise it,
                vibrate with it.

When I say, "Be at peace,"
or "Be still and know that I am God,"
    are they just words to you,
        lovely comforting words?

Do you find yourself surrounded with that peace so that nothing disturbs you?

Do you find yourself being perfectly still,
and find the truth in those words, "I am God"?
    They are such tremendous words,
    the most powerful words that were ever spoken.

When you realize they are living words,
when you fully realize the power of those words,
    you will find that you have reached and know the meaning
    of having dominion over all things.
    As you repeat those words over and over again
    they become part of you.

You find that when you are very disturbed or restless
    and you repeat to yourself, "Be at peace, be at peace,"
        slowly a sense of peace begins to spread over you;
        and the more you go on saying it
        the more you feel yourself become one with that peace.

Repetition is a good thing
    and very necessary until you finally have absorbed a certain truth
        and it has become a part of your living—
            which you will find is what eventually happens.

So when you find I am repeating Myself to you over and over again,
do not become impatient
but realize that I do this because you have not yet absorbed fully
what I am telling you,
    that the words have not yet become living words to you
    and you have not started to vibrate with them.

I have infinite patience
and I will never cease from bringing home My truths to you
    until finally they are a part of you
    and you are living them all the time in your daily living.

I have set My hand upon you,
    I have chosen you to do a specific work for Me,
        therefore I will not let you go.

    Very patiently,
    very lovingly,
I go on and on instructing you,
        leading you,
            guiding you.

I know your deepest longing is to do My will,
and that is one of the greatest steps in the right direction.
As long as you have that desire to do My will
I can always reach you.

I tell you from time to time
    that time is getting short
    and there is much to be done,
    that time must not be wasted in doing unguided things,
    that everything you do must be done with My blessings.

Take all this to heart
even though you do not quite know what I mean by time;
    at least let this knowledge keep you ever alert and on your toes
        so you live fully in the now
            giving of your very best,
                following out My instructions to the letter.

No man knows what tomorrow may bring,
therefore live to the full in the glorious *now.*

As you search diligently
you will surely find what you are looking for:
    your at-one-ment with Me
    the source of all life
    all good;
but you have to take time to search.

This is something that will not drop into your laps without the deep
desire in you to know Me,
                to know the truth,
                    to seek until you find what this really means to you.

This deep spiritual experience of inner knowing comes only to those
who really want to know.
Therefore never just dabble vaguely in these spiritual experiences;
  realize that once you have started on this quest
    nothing will satisfy you
      until you have found what you are looking for,
        your at-one-ment with Me.

This is something each individual has to do on his own.
  Someone may be able to point the way to you,
    but it is up to you to do the rest,
      it is up to you to go forth
        and experience it within.

Until you start to put what you are learning into practice,
you really do not know whether it works for you or not.
  It may work for others,
  but what about you?
    What does it mean to you to live by faith
      unless you do something about it
      and put it to the test?

Remember you cannot bask in someone else's deep inner spiritual experiences.
  It helps to read about them
  to learn about them
  and even to hear and talk about them;
but it is up to you to live them
and practise them in your own lives
if you desire to live by the spirit,
to live by faith.

You all know this
but what are you doing about it?
  Are you just hearers of the word,
  or are you doers of it?

No one can make you live this life;
every soul is absolutely free to make his own choice.
                What have you chosen?

Just sit back
and spend the rest of your life listening to other people's experiences?
  or are you going to start right here and now
    living a life fully dedicated to Me,
      to My work,

putting into practice all those wonderful lessons you have been learning,
and seeing how they really do work?

How completely empty and futile life is
   until you start living it to the full
      and putting everything to the test
to see whether this spiritual life really is practical and worth living.

Start right now doing something about it,
waste no more time talking about it;
      there is far too much talk
      and not nearly enough action.

Let there be no armchair spirituality;
   let it be living,
   and vibrating,
   there for all to see.
Let Me see you start living a life *now.*

When you are in tune,
   in harmony with all life
      you will find that nothing can harm you
         because you blend in perfectly with the whole
            and you are master of the whole situation.

It is when you are out of harmony
   and there is resistance in you
      that you become the slave
         and therefore open yourselves up to negative forces.

In fact,
it is that which you fear that you draw to you
and become overwhelmed by.

Fear nothing.
There is nothing to fear when you are at one with all life.
That is why I constantly remind you to be ever aware of Me
and of My divine presence.
     When your whole being is filled with light and love
     there is no room for any negativity;
     for light and darkness cannot abide together
     any more than love and fear.
Perfect love casts out all fear.

Whatever you undertake,
no matter how seemingly impossible or heavy the task may be,
    do it fearlessly
    with the knowledge that you are not doing it on your own,
    but that I am with you always.
    I will show you the way
and show you exactly how to handle the whole situation so that it will
fall into place and work out perfectly.

Never allow any doubts in
and never look back.
    Simply know that what you have undertaken is right
    and that only the very best will come out of it.
Go ahead in faith
and do what you know has to be done
and see perfect results.

How can you expect things to go right
and to go smoothly
    when you are full of doubts
    and riddled with fear?
You immediately put up a barrier
creating the wrong conditions
so bringing about failure.
It is all your own doing,
    so never look around for a scapegoat to blame
       but look within yourself
          and recognize where you have gone wrong
            and then do something about it.

Never be satisfied to wallow in your failures and mistakes
    and be dragged down by self pity.
Miserable is the man who is sorry for himself
    and allows self pity to creep into his life
       and dominate it.

See your mistakes and failures;
 learn by them,
 be determined not to make the same mistakes again,
 then move on;
giving thanks for all the wonderful things life has endowed you with:
  for life
   for health
    for beauty all around you
     for friends
      for the very breath you breathe
      for everything
      everything.
Realize more and more how mightily blessed you are
and how much you have to be grateful for.
As you do so,
 all feelings of self and self pity will disappear completely,
  because your hearts are full of love and gratitude
   and you are in tune with Me
   and all is very, very well.

Unite,
 unite,
  unite.
When there is unity
there is nothing to hold up the manifestation of that which is on the
etheric, and it can be brought about at great speed.

Search your hearts.
Is there anything in any of you
 which is causing disunity and division,
  which is holding up the manifestation of the next phase of the work?
Is there any misunderstanding,
 jealousy,
  envy,
   or anything negative which may be putting on the brakes?

This is something each one of you will have to seek and find out deep within.
It is not something to be discussed or pulled to pieces.
It does mean that all will have to face themselves fairly and squarely
and really be honest with themselves.
You will know without a shadow of doubt if you happen to be that piece
of grit which is holding up the perfect outworking of My plan.

When you have faced up to it
    you can do something about it:
        you can seek My cleansing and purifying
        and once again get into tune and harmony with the whole
        and find that unity and oneness.

Do not sit back
and point your finger at anyone else;
    simply take time to be still
        and in the stillness look within your own heart.
If you find a great sense of peace and harmony within
you have nothing to be concerned about;
    but if you feel uncomfortable
        and find yourselves making excuses
            and trying to justify your actions and your thoughts,
you may be sure there is something deep within you that needs to be changed.

When you recognize this
    do not allow it to concern you and weigh you down
        but start right there and then
            to change your whole outlook and attitude.

I am always there to help you;
    do not try to do it on your own.
Call on Me
    and I will answer you
        and help you to overcome all that seems to stand in your way
            preventing you from feeling at one with the whole.

There is so much on the etheric which is waiting to be manifested
in form on the physical;
    wonder upon wonder,
        miracle upon miracle.
Again I say,
    unite
        and help to bring this about without any further delay.
            Allow nothing in you to hold it up.

Let not à thought of the self
   or of what you want for the self
      mar the plan.

Think only for the whole,
  plan for the whole,
    work for the whole,
      give to the whole
and so help really to speed things up.

The perfect plan is there—
you help to bring it about.

Let Me fill your heart,
          mind,
               soul, and being
with the beauty and harmony of all life.
It is there all around you
              and within you.
Wake up to it,
  wake up
    and enjoy it to the full
      and give eternal thanks for it.

A life filled with beauty and harmony is a joy to behold;
it radiates and projects law
            and order
                and perfect rhythm
                   and harmony.

A true work of art
whatever it may be,
must have balance,
          grace,

harmony,
and order.
A beautiful soul reflects these qualities for all to see.
Have I not told you many times that that which is within is reflected without?

When there is chaos and confusion within
it is reflected without by a life of chaos and confusion
and it cannot be hidden.
So with peace,
harmony,
beauty,
love—
they are reflected in your outer living and appearance.

To get into rhythm with life you have to learn the art of being still.
The stiller you can become
the clearer can you reflect the qualities of your soul.

How easy it is to blame your environment,
your situation,
your conditions for the state you are in.
How nice it is to have something or someone else to blame,
to have a scapegoat.
It is high time you ceased doing this
and realized that you have only yourselves to blame for the state you are in,
that when you can seek and find that inner peace and stillness
nothing and no one without will be able to disturb it
or throw you off balance.

Look around you,
look at the beauty and perfection of nature:
everything in nature is in rhythm,
there is perfect law and order in My universe,
nothing is out of tune,
there is a time and reason for everything.
It is all there for all to see
and for all to partake of,
so get into tune with it,
flow with it
and be part of that law and order in My universe.

Are you not part of the whole?
Then why separate yourselves by living a disordered chaotic life?
As you fill your minds with beautiful thoughts,
say beautiful words

and accomplish beautiful things,
so do you become one with the beautiful wholeness which is My universe,
    which is Me
        and everything fits in perfectly.

Take time to reflect on this,
    and get into tune,
        and into harmony,
            and do it now.

As each individual seeks and finds that inner peace and harmony
so will peace and harmony reign in the world.
It has to start somewhere;
    so why not let it start in you
                        and you
                            and you,
and realize that you, by doing your part, can help to bring peace and
harmony into the world.

It is every tiny drop of water that makes up the mighty ocean;
    and every tiny grain of sand that makes up the beach;
        so every individual at peace within can bring peace without into the world.
        So why not do your part?

Expand your consciousness
and know that I am all there is.
Then go on and on expanding it
    and see the all-inclusiveness of the I AM
        and see clearly that you are the I AM of the I AM,
            that there is no place where I am not.

Keep stretching,
    feel every atom in you ache with stretching,

feel yourselves growing,
     breaking all bonds which have held you in bondage
     and have stifled your growth and expansion.

As a tiny seed planted in the earth breaks its outer skin
   and begins to grow
                 and expand
                         and develop into that which it really is,
so let your real self grow and expand
   until you become what you really are
   and behold the beauty and wonder of it all.

As you do so
   know that you are one with all life,
      now and forever;
that never again can you be separated from this,
   that I am in you
      and you are in the I AM.

As you take time in the stillness
   and allow this to be absorbed into your being
                        to become a very part of you,
you will begin to find a new freedom in life,
you will begin to really live and move and have your being in the
                        wholeness of the whole,
you will find yourselves in your true environment.
You will be able to do all things,
you will know that absolutely nothing is impossible
   for it is the I AM who is working in and through you,
      and when I am recognized
         and accepted
            anything is possible.

Can you feel yourselves expanding now?
   Can you accept all that I am saying to you?
      Or are you still full of doubts and fears,
      afraid to step out into the unknown,
      to accept the truth
      and know that the truth will set you free?

I can keep on imparting these wonderful truths to you,
   but unless you are willing to accept them
      and use them in your lives and living
         they will do you no good.
They improve with constant use.

What are you going to do about them?
It is up to you to take action.
You must have faith,
for know you not that according to your faith be it unto you?
You must believe,
for without belief you hold up the manifestation of all My good and
perfect gifts which I am holding out to you.
Unless a gift which is held out to you is accepted with grace and gratitude
it cannot benefit you.
Therefore let not pride nor false humility stop you from accepting
that which is your rightful heritage.

All that I have is yours
when you can accept your oneness with Me,
without any reservations.
Do this in that risen state of consciousness where you know the truth
of the I AM within you.

When you listen to My voice
it is the most natural thing in the world to you.
It has become as natural to you as breathing;
there is no strain about it whatsoever.
That is the way I want it to be.

It should never be necessary for you to come into a special state
before you can hear My voice.
You should be able to hear it at all times and in all places
no matter what is happening around,
no matter what state you may be in—
your need for Me is constant.
As it was in the beginning
when man walked and talked with Me,
so it is happening again now.

Think on these things.
    This is the most wonderful relationship any soul could ask for,
    and this, I want you to know, anyone can have,
    this is the relationship I long to have with all My children.

Only the lower self prevents this happening.
You know this,
    because if there is ever a blockage between us
        it is never anything to do with Me.
            I never withdraw Myself from My children.
They withdraw themselves from Me
by allowing the lower self to step into the way.

Each of you functions in different ways;
    therefore never compare,
        keep your heart open,
            and your understanding,
                and seek Me at all times.

Listen to the birds,
                singing My songs of praise,
and let your heart be full of joy and thanksgiving
and sing My praises forever.

My works are mighty.
    My ways are wonderful.
        Let Me work in and through each one of you.
    Cooperate with life,
    go with it
    and do not fight against it.

Beyond all else, learn to get your values right

and put first things first.
    I have told you many times:
        you cannot expect everything to drop straight into your lap
        unless you do your part
        and put first things first.
It is time you learned this lesson,
for it is a fundamental one.

Stop for a moment in all your busy-ness
and see what you are putting first:
    Is it work?
    Is it living?
    Is it your wants?
    Your desires?
"Seek ye first My kingdom."
    Get into tune with Me,
        find your direct contact with Me
            and all else shall be added unto you.

Do you not realize that your communion with Me means far more than
anything else,
for it is from this contact that all else stems.

I am the source,
    and until you realize this,
        accept it,
            and draw from it,
                things do not happen.

You cannot draw water from a well
    unless you get a bucket
        and let it down on a rope into the well,
            fill it with water
                and then draw it up.
    You have to do something,
    you have to make the effort
    and do your part.
Standing at the top of the well looking at the water will not draw it up.

So with this spiritual life;
standing around watching others using the laws of manifestation will
not make them work for you.
Seeing others find their oneness with Me will not do it for you.

Every soul has to do its own inner seeking and finding.

All have to do their own inner work,
   their own thinking,
      make their own inner contact
         and stand on their own feet.

No one can live on someone else's glory,
no one can live someone else's life for them.
   You cannot be lazy spiritually,
   you must do something about it.
   Really see it work in your lives and living.
It does work,
for all you have to do is to open your eyes
and you will see how truly wonderfully it works
in the lives of those who truly love Me
and put Me first in everything.

Why not take time to be still
   and go into the silence,
      study your motives
         and see whether they are of the highest?

What are you doing about the things that really matter in life?
Have you got your values right?
   Only you can do this for yourselves,
      no one else can do it for you,
         and it does take time and patience.
It may even mean waiting upon Me
without receiving an immediate answer.
   You may have important lessons to learn
      which you can only learn in this way
         by being still and waiting upon Me,
especially if you are an impatient and demanding soul.

Why make excuses for yourselves?
You know all the answers in theory:
   now it is time you put them into practice
   and see how they work for you
   not just for others.

You will never learn these vitally important lessons
   until you put them to the test themselves.
   Why not do it now
and stop wasting time thinking about them?

Be still,
    be very still
        and know that I am God,
            that I am within you,
                around you,
                    above you,
                        below you.

I am everywhere,
I am within all things.

Expand your consciousness.
Stretch until you ache all over.

Your deepest longing and desire is to seek and find the truth;
    therefore you cannot fail to do so
        because as each soul chooses of its own free will to seek,
            so will it find.
Every book you pick up to read throws a little more light on what
you are seeking.

You do not have to seek very far for the answer
for the answer lies within your very being.
    You seek Me,
    I am within.
        You seek the truth,
        the truth is within.
            You seek joy and happiness;
            that joy and happiness are not without,
            again you will find them within.
                You seek love,
                that love is within.
All the treasures of heaven are within your very being.

Stop seeking,
    but instead unlock the door
        and step right into that world within
            and there you will find all that you desire.
Nothing will be withheld from you,
for all is yours as soon as you become aware of it.

Is it not wonderful to know that your seeking days are over?
Now it is simply a case of unwrapping each gift which you find within,
with the greatest of care,
studying each gift,
and then putting it to good use.

These gifts,
     all of them,
          are there to be used
               and constantly used.

Never keep them to the self,
     never hide them;
     bring them forth and use them,
they improve with use.

As priceless pearls, when they are shut up in velvet caskets,
become sick from lack of wear
and have to be brought out into the light of day
and placed around the neck of a person to bring them to full
life and glory again,
so with each gift.
     Bring it out into the light so all can see,
          hide nothing.

You know you are one with Me;
     therefore live that oneness,
     demonstrate it in your everyday living.
Do not just display it on high days and holidays
but all the time.

You have within you the gift of My divine love;
     let it shine forth in action.
There is no use talking about My divine love
     if you do not live it
          and demonstrate it in your living.

You feel happy;
     well, let that happiness reflect in your whole being,
          for that happiness stems from within.
Open the door and let it out.
     You cannot say how happy you are
          and then go around with a long face and gloomy expression.
It must be expressed in your whole being.
Live happiness.

So with every gift you find within.
Unwrap it and put it to its full use.
    That is the way you can live a full and glorious life,
    that is the way you can demonstrate that I am indeed one with you,
    that I am indeed within you.
Let us live that life together and in complete at-one-ment.

SERVICE

I was shown a casket filled with wonderful jewels and precious stones.

Then I saw the lid snapped shut, the key turned in the lock, and the casket carefully put away into a very strong safe.

I heard the words: "All My good and perfect gifts are there to be used, not to be put away for safekeeping. Why not open the doors of your hearts, and use them to My honour and glory."

Step by step let the way open up,
   with no feeling of strain or stress.
      All is in My hands,
      all has My blessings,
      there is a pattern and plan running through all that is happening.
Go ahead in absolute confidence,
   and do what has to be done.

Keep your heart open so My divine love can pour through it.
Every soul needs to be assured of this.

Never feel you have nothing to give:
   you have the most precious gift in all the universe to give
      for you are a channel for My divine love.
         Mankind is hungry for it,
         the need in the world for it is tremendous.

You feel that it is so often misunderstood:
this is so.
But do not let this concern you.
   You are My channel,
   My instrument,
   and as such you need only do My will.
Never concern yourself regarding the reaction or effect it may have on anyone.

I ask you to say something,
   to write something;
      you obey My voice.
The outcome may be very different to your own conception of what it
                    ought to be.
Never mind.
Simply know and understand that it is only when I have implicit obedience
to My word that miracles can be brought about.
You simply do what I ask you to do
and then leave the rest to Me.

When a soul is ready I can work in them.
The seeds of love never fall on barren ground.
   They may lie dormant for some time,

but eventually when conditions are ready
        they will burst forth
            and flower
                and flourish.

So,
you plant the seeds
and at the right time I will tend those seeds.

All is very well.
The work that is being done here is now bringing forth much fruit;
    you will behold the wonder and glory of it
    and will lift up your heart
    and glorify Me
    and see My hand in all that has been happening.

It is a wonderful time,
    a really thrilling time;
        open your eyes and behold it
and realize that you are part of it.

It is not necessary to try too hard to become perfect;
simply hold before you the vision of My perfection
    and know that that is what you are going to manifest in form,
        perfection in all things;
        for I am in all things
        and I am perfection.

Blot out discord
    and see only harmony all around you;
blot out imperfection,
    and see only perfection.

You can do it
and you can do it instantly
without wasting any time wondering whether it is possible.

With Me all things are possible,
    and I am within the very centre of your being.
        I am that I am.
Vibrate from that tremendous statement,
and as you do so you raise your vibrations
and see the ordinary things in life in a completely different light.
    You begin to see a real sparkle in something which you had always
        considered so ordinary and mundane;
you begin to see life and purpose in everything around you;
you are living and vibrating in the new.

This is where life takes on a completely different hue;
    instead of everything being just black and white
        everything vibrates in colour.
You become very aware of colours,
    you become very alert to the sounds of nature all around you.
        When you work in the garden
            you become aware of tiny things you have never noticed before.
You see in the work you are doing a purpose,
a lesson to be learnt.

You were pulling up nettles one day
and you wondered how you were going to tackle a mass of them;
    then you found as you tackled each little clump as you came to it,
    you were able to pull them up
    and dispose of them quite easily.

You see how important it is to stop looking ahead,
    to just live fully in the moment
        doing what is required of you in that moment.
That is the way to get on top of things;
    if you try to look too far ahead
        you become so overwhelmed with the amount to be done
            that you want to throw up your hands and say "impossible,"
                that you are incapable of doing it.

That is why
    by living fully in the moment
    doing everything to the very best of your ability
you will be able to accomplish the seemingly impossible without even
realizing that you are doing it;

and when you look back
   and see what has been accomplished,
      you will be amazed
         and will lift up your heart in deep deep gratitude
          and give me eternal thanks.

You will see My divine hand in everything that has been accomplished
and know that indeed with Me all things are possible.

Never try to undertake too many projects
for you simply waste your energy by spreading it too thinly.
When you do this
   you are unable to do anything perfectly
     or wholeheartedly
       because when you are doing one thing your mind is on the next.

This means you have not learned that vital lesson of pinpointed concentration
which is what is essential if you wish to create something.

Stop being a butterfly,
   flitting from one project to the next,
     never completing anything,
but learn the art of concentration
and of creation.

What are you really good at?
   Search your hearts
     and find out
       and then take that gift
         and concentrate on it.

Are you good at music,

singing,
acting,
or is it painting or handicrafts,
is it cleaning,
or looking after people?

Whatever it is
and no matter how ordinary or mundane it may appear to be,
learn to concentrate on it
    and develop it.
Cease trying your hand at everything,
    dissipating your power and energy
        and failing miserably in everything as a result.

There are so many wonderful things to do in life
but realize right now that you can only do one thing at a time;
    so get on
        and do one thing at a time
            and do it wholeheartedly.

You will only be able to perfect what you are doing if you practise.
You cannot hope to be a really good musician unless you practise;
you cannot hope to be a good artist unless you take time to practise your art;
you cannot hope to be a good mother and housewife unless you
put that into practise as well.

What can you do best?
    Find out
        and then go ahead and do it
            and enjoy doing it.
Do not waste time and energy longing to do something else
    or wishing you were somewhere else with other opportunities.
Realize you are in exactly the right place at the right time
    and you are there for a specific purpose
        to do a specific job;
therefore give all you have got to that job
and do it with love and joy.

See what fun life can be not just for yourself, but also for all those
with whom you are in contact.

What deep satisfaction you will find when you do what has to be done
                                        perfectly
and when you do it for the benefit of the whole.
Unless you give of your very best to the whole

you cannot hope to become part of that whole,
    you cut yourself off from it
        and there is no wholeness in you.

Be yourselves.
"To thine own self be true."
When you are in contact with Me
    and are drawing your all from Me,
        your own self is your higher self, never the lower self.
Then you can indeed be your true self
    and live and work from a spiritual level of consciousness,
        and behold the most amazing things taking place.
            You will behold the supernatural things coming about
            because you are working with My laws
            and are in tune with all life.

As you learn to do this more and more
you will behold miracle upon miracle taking place
until you fully understand that with Me nothing is impossible.
    But you must be true to that higher self.
    You must be afraid of nothing
    and be willing to do the most unusual things without any hesitation.

Always remember that you are functioning from the spiritual,
not from the human level of consciousness.
    You are working with My laws
        not man's laws;
            and if these take you out on a limb
            go out on it without a thought of self,
            because you know that only the very best will come about.

Seek not approval

nor popularity with your fellowman
but seek always to do My will
no matter what the cost.
This will not be easy for those who choose the easy way and are
determined to have peace at any price.
I tell you peace will come
and will be lasting
when it is sought by following out My directions,
even if at the time they may appear to be unreasonable
and even foolish.

When you choose to do My will
and walk in My ways
you have to do it wholeheartedly
no matter what this may mean.

You have to take the rough with the smooth when learning the vital
lesson of instant obedience to My will.
Only when you give all
will you receive all.
In this spiritual life you cannot pick out all the plums and leave the cake.
It is a case of all or nothing.

Many souls like to choose the parts in this life that appeal to them
and to ignore those parts that do not comply with their baser desires.
This is not living a spiritual life;
this is picking and choosing what you want to do,
not what I require of you.
You cannot expect things to work out for you if that is your attitude.

I need your total surrender
and total dedication
before I can work those wonders
and miracles
in and through you.

You all know this;
so why not do something about it
and do it *now?*

"Ye shall know the truth and the truth shall set you free."

Never at any time close your hearts and minds;
never be afraid of the new,
                of the strange,
                        of the unconventional.
Be ready and prepared to listen to the intuition,
                                to the inspiration,
which may reveal something completely new to you—
something so new that it may not even have form or substance
and you may have to give it form and substance
and may have to clothe it in words.

Nothing is new in the universe,
    but much has been hidden down the ages which is now to be revealed.
It has been hidden
because man has misused it by using it for the self and for self glorification
so that all that wonderful wisdom, knowledge and power has had to be
withdrawn:
until man has learned to take nothing to the self;
until he has realized that he is nothing
    and is willing to give Me the honour and glory for everything;
until he has recognized that it is I working in and through him
    which enables him to do the work.

Take nothing to the self
    for as soon as you do that
        you block the flow of inspiration
            and I know immediately when something is being drawn to the self.
Give constant praise and thanksgiving
    for everything that is being revealed to you
        and then go forth
            and use it for the benefit of the whole:
realizing that you are but My channels,
My messengers,
and that all you receive comes from Me.

You long for the joy and freedom of the spirit:
it is yours

as soon as you accept where all your good and perfect gifts
come from,
and you acknowledge Me as the source of your all,
and accept that you are as nothing without Me.

Intellectual pride can be a handicap along this spiritual path
and can be a real strumbling block to the truth.
   It is not the intellect you need,
   it is inspiration and intuition.
      The intellect comes from without,
      whereas inspiration and intuition come from within
      and cannot be influenced by anything without.

Let your learning come from within;
      draw from all that you have within you.
         You will be amazed at what you contain:
         it is limitless
         because it comes from Me and I am limitless
         and all that is of Me is limitless and eternal.

Why not start drawing from that source right now?
      Each one of you has these wonderful potentials within you
         but there they remain
         until you choose to draw them forth
         and use them their right way.
Misuse any of My gifts
and they will be withdrawn from you.
Always remember this.

Bring down My heaven upon the Earth;
      it is up to you to do it.
      It is up to you to create heaven upon the Earth

by the way you live,
by your attitude towards life.

Life is wonderful
but you have to open your eyes
and see the wonder and glory of it.

You must be willing to see all the good things in life,
concentrate on them
and ignore the bad,
the negative,
the destructive things,
and give them no life force.

When I tell you to behold My new heaven and new earth
you have to do something about it.
They are there;
but few there are who are fully aware of them
and realize that they are there for all
not just for the select few to enjoy.
Unless you are aware of what is going on around you,
you cannot take part
and become part of it.

With the new come great changes,
and very often it is the changes that man dislikes,
with the result that he would prefer to remain with his eyes tightly shut;
to stay in the old
and know nothing about the wonderful new heaven and new earth
waiting there for him.

You only see what you want to see,
you remain blind to the rest.
You only hear what you want to hear;
all around you are the wonders and beauty of nature
and yet you can go through a whole day
without even noticing what is around you.

The tiny larks can be singing their songs of praise as they soar
higher and higher into the sky, and yet you can be completely oblivious
to the wonder of their song
unless you take time to stop
and listen
and become aware of what is happening.

What a lot you miss in life
by simply shutting it out of your consciousness,
by refusing to raise your consciousness to the state where you blend
together with all life.

Take time to stop,
                to look
                        and to listen
so that you miss nothing
    and can really enjoy everything.
        Then give eternal thanks for it all.

Start this day to create a better world around you
by all you do,
                say
                and think
and really enjoy it all to the full.

Life is there to be enjoyed
and every day should be full to overflowing with all the good things
in life.
Expect the best
and accept only the best.

You have been told this many times:
yet many of you are still content to accept second best
    either because you feel unworthy to receive the best
        or you are just too lazy to raise your consciousness
            until you visualize the very best
            and then hold the very best in your consciousness
            until it manifests in form.

This is where you have to put into practice that lesson of patience,
persistence and perseverance
and see it work out.

Give constant thanks for all My good and wonderful gifts which I pour
down upon you.
Use them all for the benefit of the whole
   and to My honour and glory
      and you will indeed find true and lasting happiness and contentment.

   By all means use them—
they have been given to you to use;
but do not let them use you,
do not become possessive of those wonderful gifts
and hold them to the self;
or you will surely lose them,
for they have been given to you to give,
                    to share,
                      to delight in the sharing.

Every soul has something to share.
   There are gifts and possessions on many different levels.
   You may not have material gifts,
but you may be sure you have other gifts whatever they are.

Hold them not to the self,
   hide them not,
      but be willing to bring them out into the open,
         uncover them
           and then use them as they should be used:
              never for the glorification of the self
              but always to My honour and glory.

Possess nothing
but use and enjoy all you have to the full.
The gifts I give you are not given to be hidden away but are there
to be used.

What have you to give?
Take time to find out, if you do not know.
     It may be something unique;
     and because it is unique you may feel it is not worthwhile sharing
     because you cannot see how it can fit into the whole.
I tell you
   every gift can be used
     and should be used fully.

This is why you have all been drawn together in this way,
why you are all so different,

so that you can all become part of the perfect whole
   as you contribute your specific gift,
   and allow it to be used for the whole,
   without a single thought of the self
   or what you can get out of it.

Give wholeheartedly
   and give with joy,
      and be grateful that you have something to give,
                              whatever it may be.
It is not necessary to let your left hand know what your right hand gives.
It is not necessary to shout about your gifts
   but very quietly to give of them
      and as you do so to see how they are needed
         and how they fit in perfectly with the whole.

Be grateful for being used in this way.
   When you have chosen to live this way of life
      completely dedicated to Me and to My work,
      you can no longer cling on to anything
      because you realize that all you have is Mine
      and therefore it is there to be shared with the whole.

How many times have you heard
or even muttered to yourselves:
   "What a mess the world is in these days!
   What a state of chaos and confusion!"

You have felt that there was nothing much you could do about it.
It seemed hopeless
   and out of your control,
      and you have hidden yourselves away in your shells like snails,

and left the world to get worse and worse.

Where is your sense of responsibility towards the state of the world?
Do you not realize:
    that what you do,
    how you live,
    how you think can help
               or hinder the state of the world?

It takes every tiny grain of sand to make up the sea shore;
    it takes every tiny drop of water to make up the ocean.
What you do with your thinking helps to make or mar the world;
have you ever thought of that?

The more souls who are thinking loving, positive, constructive thoughts
about the world,
the more you realize what a truly wonderful and beautiful world you are
living in.
    You are all very much a part of it,
    you are all a tiny part of that vast wholeness
    and you have your specific part to play.
The more quickly you realize this
the sooner will the state of the world begin to change.

Cease being drawn into the whirlpool of universal thought forms
    of chaos and confusion
    of destruction and devastation,
start right now concentrating on the wonder and beauty of the world
around you.

Give thanks for everything,
    bless all those whom you contact,
        refuse to see the worst in people,
                in things,
                   in conditions
and seek always for the very best.
Concentrate on that very best
and see the wonderful changes which will take place in the world all
around you.

You can do this
    and you can start doing it today
        in fact you can start doing it now.

This is not being like an ostrich hiding your head in the sand;

and refusing to face the realities of the world;
it is simply looking for
   and concentrating on the very best in everything and everyone.

You are a tiny world within yourself.
When there is peace,
            harmony,
                 love
                    and understanding right there,
                       deep within *your* little world,
it will be reflected on the outer,
in the world all around you.

Start putting your own house in order,
   start readjusting your thinking and living
      and stop pointing your finger at anyone else
         and spotlighting their faults and failings.
You have more than enough to do to right yourself.
When you can do that
you are beginning to help the whole vast situation in the world.

Why not start right now really to love the world you are in,
   really enjoy it to the full,
      absorb the beauties and wonders of it?

It is full of energies, of goodness.
   It is a wonderful, wonderful world
      and you are greatly blessed and privileged to be living in it.

It is up to you to bring down heaven upon earth.
   What are you doing about it?
   Stop looking to the other fellow to do something about it,
and start doing something about it yourself.

Be not hypocrites.
You cannot say you love Me and hate your fellowmen,
    for love and hate are like oil and water—
        they do not mix.

When you truly love Me
    you will love your fellowman;
    you will love one another,
    you will have compassion and understanding towards one another.
And when you love one another
you will love Me—
they are so intertwined that they cannot be separated.

Love is so strong
    yet so gentle.
Greater love hath no man than he who lays down his life for his friends.
    How great is your love for one another?
    Are you willing to put yourselves out for one another?
    Are you willing to go that second mile
    no matter how busy or how weary you are?

Love does not need to be expressed in words,
    it is seen and felt in action,
        it radiates from you—
            it *is* you.

Love is the language of silence,
    it can be understood and accepted without a word being spoken,
        it is an international language
            understood by the heart
                not by the mind.

It matters not what nationality you are,
    you can always convey love
        and communicate it in complete silence.
Your eyes,
your heart,
your attitude,
your whole being can convey what you are feeling towards one another.

When love flows freely in the hearts of all men,
    hatred, jealousy, war and dissension will be no more
        and peace will reign supreme.
Without love there can be no peace,
                        no understanding.

122

You cannot learn about love from books,
   you cannot be told about love.
      You just have to *be* love
      and open your hearts
      and let it flow.
Love stems from Me—
I am love.

Raise your consciousness,
   forget yourselves,
      think of others,
         give in service to others
            and joy and love will radiate from you.
               As you learn to give to others in service
               it opens your hearts
               and keeps them open.

The more you give freely and joyously
   the more love pours forth from you
      and the more love you draw to you.

You cannot love without being loved;
   it is a two-way thing—
   a giving and a receiving.
      The more love you give,
      the more you will receive.
This is the law.

Never be discouraged if love is not returned to you immediately.
Simply know that sooner or later it will be,
and just keep the love flowing no matter what the response may be,
for love will melt the hardest of hearts in the end.

Love never takes "no" for an answer.
Love is never defeated.
   Love is not like a snail,
   it never withdraws when it is rebuffed or rejected.
      It turns the other cheek
      and just goes on and on loving.

Can you do this?
   You cannot do it in your own strength
      but with Me you can do anything.
         Seek My help at all times
         and I will never fail you

and you will find you can love
and love
and go on loving
without any difficulty.

Your life is My life lived through you.
You are My hands and feet
and I need each one of you to work in and through.
You are all different aspects of the whole
and you are all greatly needed in your different ways.

Never withdraw yourselves
feeling that you are not needed
and that someone else can take your place.

You each have something unique to contribute to the whole,
therefore let yourselves be used.
Do your part, whatever it may be, wholeheartedly
and find your rightful place in the whole vast intricate pattern of
life.

Give eternal thanks
that you can be used in that specific way
which is your own unique way.

Have you found out what you can contribute to the whole?
Can you feel yourselves blending in, in true perfection?
Or do you still feel you are standing on the outside looking in
wondering just where you fit in?
Why not step right in
and by so doing find that special place more quickly and easily?
Once you are part of that whole
you will want to give of your very best.

You will want to find your place
and know exactly where you fit in.

Many times I have likened this to a clock with its many parts.
Every part is needed for the clock to go and to keep the right time,
and it is when each part is in its rightful place doing its specific
job that precision timing is achieved.

You cannot all be the face or the hands of the clock—
the parts that are in the forefront and are seen all the time.
Those tiny screws and cogwheels are just as important—
those springs and parts that are tucked away unseen by any except the
clock mender must be there for the clock to function.

Never try to be like someone else,
    just be yourselves
        and do your part whatever it may be.
Be not resentful because you are in the background tucked away
unnoticed by the many.
Simply realize that in your own quiet way you are greatly needed
for the smooth running of the whole.

Do all that you have to do with your whole heart
    and really enjoy doing it.
        Find real joy in seeing the smooth running of the whole
            and know that you are doing your part to help bring it about.

Every soul longs to be wanted,
    to be really needed.
        When you feel needed
            you begin to grow
                and to flower and flourish
                    and give of your very best.

Always remember that I have need of you;
    so offer yourselves anew to Me each day
        that I can use you as I will,
            and grow in strength and stature.

Shoulder your responsibilities joyously, whatever they may be.
    Life is a real joy,
        wake up and realize this.
        You are mightily blessed,
            realize this too.

Take absolutely nothing for granted,
    for when you do life goes dead on you
        and all the joy goes out of it.
Give constant thanks for everything
and really count those blessings.

Do what you know you have to do to My honour and glory
and therefore do it perfectly.

"Do unto others as you would have them do unto you."

No one likes to be hurt or slighted,
    no one likes to be ignored
        or made to feel unloved and unwanted.
So why not treat your fellowman with love and respect.
    Try to understand him
    and be willing to go that second mile with him if necessary.
    Be very tolerant,
    very patient and very loving.
This is the way you would like to be treated yourselves,
so live as you would wish others to live.

Be an example
and see that it is a really good example;
        but never do it because you feel it is expected of you,
        do it because you really want to do it, and long with all your heart
        to give of your highest and best in everything you do, say and think.
The greater your desire
the easier it will be to fulfil it.

Never be satisfied with anything mediocre
    or half-hearted,
        see that everything you do is of the very highest,

that your motives are pure
and that there is nothing selfish or self centred in anything you do.

Take time to search your hearts
and find out why you are doing what you are doing
and why you are where you are
and then answer yourselves truthfully.

It is important at this time that you are in the right place
doing the right thing
for these are crucial times.
So much is taking place on many levels
and each soul is needed in its rightful place.
It is like a vast jigsaw puzzle being put together,
there is a right place for every tiny piece.

Are you in your rightful place?
Only you will know.
Do you feel comfortable with the vibrations?
Do you feel you blend in perfectly with the whole:
that you do not create any jarring or discordant note,
doing what you are doing
and living where you are living?

You must be prepared for a tremendous release of light
and if you are not prepared
it will throw you off balance.

Peace,
harmony,
tranquillity must be within you,
to stabilize you
and bring you into alignment with what is about to take place.

Therefore it is necessary to be still
and find that peace within so that nothing and no one can disturb it.
Hold on to it no matter what is taking place without.

Be like anchors,
strong and steady,
sunk deep within,
immovable so that no storm without can affect you
or shift you from your rightful place.

Hold fast,
and know that all is very very well,

that all is proceeding according to My perfect plan.

How wondrous are My ways;
    walk thou in them
        and know that no harm can befall those who do so.

Let not your hearts be troubled
    but put your whole trust, faith and security in Me
        and go your way in peace,
            doing what you know has to be done.
Let Me guide and direct your every step.

You are all members of one body,
    all parts of the whole,
        and each have your part to play in the whole.

Be not critical
    nor intolerant of one another;
        but realize that no two of you are the same,
            nor have you all the same function,
                that it takes many different parts to make up the perfect whole.

Have you ever seen a clock taken to pieces?
    There are many different parts that make up that clock;
    and as you see them lying there before you
    you wonder how they could ever make up a perfect timepiece.

But when someone who knows something about clocks takes each piece
and puts it in its rightful place
    you find that not only does it go
    but it tells the correct time.
        As long as each tiny piece remains in its rightful place
        playing its part,

everything goes smoothly.

Now you know why it is that I keep telling you to find your rightful
place in the whole vast scheme of life
and when you have found it, to give of your very best.
Do not waste time pulling your neighbour to pieces and finding fault
with him;
you really have more than enough to do to keep yourself on the straight
and narrow path without finding fault with others.

There are so many different paths to the centre,
    and when all are headed in the same direction they must be right,
        all must feel free to tread the path of their own choosing
and none should be pushed into one that does not appeal to him.

All souls have free will,
    what they do with that free will is up to them.
        They can direct it into the light
            and follow the light,
                or they can choose the way of darkness
                    and grope their way in that.
It is simply up to each individual.

That divine spark is within each individual
    but it needs to be drawn out
        and fanned into a flame in so many souls.
        It has to be recognized before anything can be done with it.
Wake up from your slumbers,
recognize the divinity within you;
nurture it and allow it to grow and flourish.

A seed has to be planted in the soil before it can grow.
    It has within it all its potentials,
        but those potentials remain dormant
until they are given the right conditions in which to grow and develop.

You each have within you the kingdom of heaven;
    but unless you wake up to the fact
        and start searching for it
            you will not find it,
                and there it will remain.

There are many souls in this life who will not wake up to this fact,
    and they are like seeds stored away in packets.

You must want to break your bonds,
    to be free.
As soon as the desire is there
    you will receive help in every possible way;
but the desire in you must be there.

Can you accept that you have within you
    all power,
    all wisdom,
    all understanding?
Or is this still theory to you?

Are you still just hearers of My word but not doers?
    Do you really want to be a power in the world,
        do you want to be able to help and uplift?

Then you must learn to be true to the very highest within you.
You will not only have to accept but know without a shadow of doubt
that I am within you
and that I can do all things.
        Nothing is impossible with Me
        and with this inner knowing
        you can be master of every situation
        and rise above anything that would stand in your way.

Learn to act from that inner voice
    and do not allow yourselves to be influenced by outer conditions
        nor by those around you.
It is so much easier to follow the crowd
    rather than follow your own individual path
        knowing that it is right for you.
It needs inner strength and conviction to enable you to do this,

130

and this is something each individual will have to seek
and find within himself.

Never be pig-headed and obstinate—
that is not being strong and confident,
acting from that inner knowing and conviction;
it is simply trying to assert an outer power and authority
which leads to dictatorship and slavery
and no good can come out of that.

When you know that something is right for you
there is no need to try and convince anyone or yourselves;
but be strong and of good courage,
go ahead doing it very quietly and unobtrusively
allowing nothing and no one to try and turn you off course.
Retain that perfect balance deep within,
then nothing can touch you.

Draw from the infinite source of power and strength within,
and you will find yourselves doing seemingly supernatural things
simply because you are working with My divine laws.

When you are doing that, anything can happen
for My laws are the keys that open all doors
and make all things possible.

Recognize them as My laws
and never fail to give eternal thanks for them
and use them to My honour and glory
and for the benefit of the whole.
Then only the most wonderful things can come out of their right use
and all shall benefit from them.

Power used aright under My guidance can change the course of history,
creating the new heaven and the new earth,
bringing life,
life,
and more life.

Used wrongly it can bring only devastation and destruction.

Power is something that must not be played with
but must be treated with great respect;
the way you respect the power of electricity
which can be a great help and benefit to mankind when used aright,
but when wrongly used can destroy and bring devastation.

I am power.
 I hold all creation in My hand
 and you are all part of that whole.
Blend with it
and find your rightful place in it.

I am the first and the last,
the beginning and the end.
I am in everything and everyone.
There is nowhere where I am not.
Tune in to the I AM of the universe
 and be at one with all life
 and start doing it now.

Be of one heart,
 one mind,
 one spirit.

Find perfect peace and harmony within
 and reflect it without.
 Peace starts within.
It is there within every soul
like a tiny seed waiting to germinate,
 and grow,
 and flourish.
 It has to be given the right conditions,
 the right environment,
 the right treatment
before it can start doing this.

Be still and create the right conditions;
be still and give it a chance to take root.

Once it is established it will continue to grow,
but in its tender beginnings it needs to be helped
    and cherished.

You hold the key to world peace within,
therefore start using that key correctly right now.
    It is stiff
    and the lock is rusty from lack of use;
        pour the oil of love into it
        and start to turn it.
It may take time to lubricate it so that it can turn with ease,
but the more love it gets
the more easily it will turn.

Do not waste time looking at the chaos and confusion in the world
but start putting it right within yourselves.
    Quietly go about doing My will.
    You do not have to talk about it but simply live it.
    Transform the chaos and confusion in your own lives
            to peace,
                serenity,
                    tranquillity
and become a useful member of society and the world you live in.
Start with yourselves
where you know you can do something,
and then work outward.

Far too many souls waste time and energy blaming the wrongs in the
world on to everyone else instead of recognizing that they can do
something about it when they start within themselves.
Start putting your own house in order first,
then you can help your neighbour.

When a stone is thrown into the centre of a pond,
    the ripples go out and out
        but they start from that stone,
            they start from that centre.
Start with yourself,
then you can radiate peace,
                love,
                    harmony,
                        understanding
    out to all around you.

Go into action now,

133

there is no better time than the present.
You long to see changes,
then start changing yourselves.
You long to see a better world, a better society,
then do something about it
not by pointing your finger at everyone else
but by looking within;
searching your own hearts,
righting your own wrongs,
finding the answer within yourselves.
Then you can move forward, with authority,
and be a real help to your neighbour,
and to all those you contact.

Change starts with the individual,
goes out into the group,
the community,
the town,
the nation,
the world.
Wholeness within creates wholeness without.
Seek and find that wholeness,
that oneness,
that union with all life;
as you seek you will find
for you will find Me in everything
and great will be the rejoicing.

Learn to appreciate and really care for all that is given to you.
Learn to be good stewards of all My good and perfect gifts.
You will only do this when you learn to take the whole on your hearts

and realize that all you have comes from Me.
Therefore you long to cherish and care for everything.

When living in a community
   this is a vitally important lesson to learn
      and yet a very difficult one,
especially when you fail to shoulder your responsibilities
as they should be shouldered.

Realize that until those important lessons of caring for and looking
after all I have given you have been learned
no more will be given.

Freely do I give to you
but stewardship of all I give you is essential.
This means that your attitude towards everything that is here must be right,
   that nothing is taken for granted,
   that there is no demand in any of you,
   that each one learns to look after everything that he uses,
   from the smallest thing to the biggest;
      that when something needs mending or maintenance
      you personally see that it is done
      and do not just leave it for someone else to do
      and shelve your responsibilities.
         If you cannot do it yourselves
         find the right person to do it
         and ask for his help.

Take time to ponder on your attitude towards everything you have
and everything you are given:
   very often when something is easily obtained
      adequate care is not given to it
         and real care is not taken
because you do not feel it belongs to you personally.

This attitude has to change,
   especially as you live in a community.
What you have comes from Me,
   it is a gift from Me, your Beloved.
When you truly love the giver
you will really cherish the gift.
Do you not realize this?
   When you fail to look after My gifts
      it reflects your attitude towards Me
         the giver of all those gifts.

Love is the key to all this:
    love for Me,
        love for the whole,
            love for each other,
                love for everything.
When you really know the meaning of love
you will never again fail to love and care for all your charge.

You do not give a child a valuable piece of equipment to play with
    because you know that child will not look after it
        and will probably destroy it.

I cannot give you all that is waiting to be given to you
    until you learn to look after it
        and use it the way it should be used—
            with love and care.

Therefore I have to wait patiently until you are ready
    before I can give you more and more of My gifts.

I have told you many times
    that all My good and perfect gifts are yours,
        in fact that all I have is yours;
        but I have always added:
"When you have learned to love Me and put Me first in everything."
    I say this because only then will I know that you will really look
    after everything the way it should be looked after.

NUTSHELLS

Joy
great joy I bring you this day
   as you watch My perfect pattern unfold
      like a glorious flower in the rays of the sun;
leaf by leaf you will behold its beauty and its perfection,
   and you will lift up your heart to the true glory of it
      and sing a song of deep praise and glory and thanksgiving for all you see.

There is something tremendous happening at this time
   and you are part of what is happening.

You are one of the actors in the play
   and you must be ready to take your part when you get your cue.

Seek within and you will find the answer.
Truth is like a many sided diamond:
    every side belongs to the whole
     but it all depends where you are as to just how you view it.
       Every soul views truth from different angles.
There is a time along the pathway of every soul
when it has to stand alone before Me
and find the I AM within with no help or guidance or support from
                anyone else.

I want you to stop for a moment
and think of a butterfly emerging from the comfort and security of its
chrysalis.
Supposing the butterfly stopped in its process of emerging and said:
        "No, I cannot leave this place,
        I don't know what lies outside this place."
Suppose it stopped and refused to move out,
what would happen?
It would be failing in its own evolution,
and if it remained in its chrysalis it would simply shrivel up and die.

So with you!
To refuse to move on
because you are afraid of the unknown
would most certainly hold up your evolution.

Love opens up a new world around you.
When you love, your vision expands and is magnified.
When you look at a flower with love,
    you see the true beauty of it;
        it is not just a flower
        but part of My wonderful creation,
        part of the whole.
You know the meaning of Oneness.

Every time you stop and say "Thank you, Beloved,"
    you are aware of Me.
Every time you behold the beauties of nature and you glory in them,
    you are aware of Me.
Every time you feel your heart opening up and love flowing to a soul,
    you are aware of Me.

Raise your consciousness continually
until you are ever conscious of Me and of My presence
and you really understand that I am within the very centre of your being,
        that there is no separateness,
            that we are One;
and then never let your consciousness stray away from that awareness.

There has to be a complete working in harmony with each of you.
   No player can become "bolshie" in an orchestra
      and allow personal likes and dislikes towards the conductor to come in
         and because of these personal feelings throw down their instrument
            and refuse to play.

That is why perfect understanding is necessary to create perfect harmony
and all the personal must go.
This is a fact
and it will be achieved
but it means a real stretching on all your parts to achieve it.

It is practice that makes perfect.
Without practice
you will be unable to perfect anything.
   A musician has to practise
      and practise
         to reach concert standard;
      an artist has to practise
         to reach professional standard;
      an athlete has to practise
         to reach Olympic standard;
therefore to reach a perfect spiritual life
   you have to live a life
      and practise it
         day in
            and day out.

Every organ in the body has its rightful place,
    and when it is functioning as it should
        the body is whole and perfect.
Every soul has a rightful place in the whole scheme of things,
    and as each one gives what it has to give to the whole
        the work moves forward in true perfection
            and there is harmony and beauty and rhythm everywhere.
Live for the whole,
think for the whole,
give to the whole,
work for the whole;
so feel part of the whole
    and become part of it
        that there is no separation.
All is working in perfect unison and harmony.

Find your own path
and tread it with absolute faith and confidence.
    It is foolishness to try and walk in someone else's footsteps
    and try to imitate them in what they are doing.
Until you know your own special path
    you will try one path after another—
        seeking,
            seeking,
                always seeking;
but when you eventually find your path
nothing and no one will be able to turn you from it,
    and that path will carry you to the ultimate goal:
    your realization of oneness with Me.

Take time this day to be still
and find out what you have to give.
Realize it takes all sorts to make the whole.

It takes all the tiny screws and cogs and springs to make a watch,
and every tiny piece has to fit into its place perfectly
and has to work with precision;
one thing out of alignment
and the whole thing is thrown out.

See that you all fit into your rightful places
and work perfectly
and in harmony and rhythm.

Real joy comes from giving
and finding your rightful place.

Far too many souls are satisfied to sit down
   and accept what others have to say
      instead of seeking for the truth within themselves.
They prefer to read and study other teachings
   instead of finding those deep spiritual truths and teachings
      deep within themselves.

Every soul is the microcosm of the macrocosm.
Every soul has all it needs deep within.

Start right now
drawing from that infinite eternal source
which knows no beginning and no end.

It is only as you practise living in My presence,
as you take time to be alone with Me
and listen to My still small voice
and obey it
    that you begin to understand the wonder of your oneness with Me,
        and you begin to bring down My heaven upon earth for all to see.
Talking about it does not do it,
    living and demonstrating it does.

A tiny spark can start off a tremendous blaze.
A small thing shared with another soul can bring light and comfort
where there was only darkness and despair.

Act on those inner promptings which come from within
and never hesitate
for they may be that tiny spark
    which will ignite something
        within a soul in very great need.

Release love into every situation
   and see what happens.
To release love:
   you have to fill your consciousness
         with loving,
           positive,
              constructive thoughts;
   you have to transform every seeming negative situation
     into a positive one—
          but
            do it quickly.

When you see a plant wilting and dying for lack of water
   and you immediately give it a drink
     you can see a change in it straight away.
So with relationships:
   when you see them strained and wilting
     apply immediately the water of My divine love
       and watch a complete transformation take place.